Charles Eugene Banks

Sword and Cross, and Other Poems

Charles Eugene Banks

Sword and Cross, and Other Poems

ISBN/EAN: 9783337254193

Printed in Europe, USA, Canada, Australia, Japan

Cover: Foto ©Thomas Meinert / pixelio.de

More available books at **www.hansebooks.com**

SWORD AND CROSS

Sword and Cross

and Other Poems

BY

CHARLES EUGENE BANKS,
CO-AUTHOR OF
"IN HAMPTON ROADS."

CHICAGO AND NEW YORK:
RAND, McNALLY & COMPANY,
PUBLISHERS.

PREFACE

COLUMBIA

While mortal monarchs one and all,
Are blindly groping to their fall,
America, behold thy queen
Survey her broad domain serene,
Move all unguarded where she will
A subtle essence none may kill.
Though balked ambition, mounting high,
Slay openly, or secretly
Drop poison to the loving cup
Of trusting rival come to sup;
Though every crown of every clime
Come tumbling down (O happy time!)
Though death claim all the heirs that purr
About the courts—what is't to her?
She 'smiles at steel and drug intense,
Immortal—nature's recompense
For banished throne and lordly train—
A goddess born of soul and brain,
A child of meditative thought,
A floating vision fancy-caught,
A rapture blown into a reed,
Columbia, a queen indeed!

CONTENTS.

CONTENTS

CONTENTS

SWORD AND CROSS

SWORD AND CROSS

Thought makes for freedom! Who is free?
  The wise, and he alone,
For wisdom hath a kindly heart,
  While ignorance is stone.

The wond'rous World is compassed by
  The clear-eyed soul that knows
It hath no master save itself—
  Free as the wind that blows.

While free men sacrifice to give
  A fettered slave release
Humanity will upward march
  Toward universal Peace.

We know not if the future hold
  The bliss for which we sigh,
But Truth is an eternal force,
  And Mercy cannot die.

Now thought goes back on swallow wings
  To that momentous morn
In June of Seventeen-Seventy-Six—
  That day our flag was born!

All beautiful upon the breeze
  It ran along the sky—
A thousand rifles welcome cried
  And cannons roared reply.

The sunbeams came in haste to kiss
  Its virgin colors whirled
In joy aloft—God's gracious sign
  That Right should rule the world.

Stern, rugged sires and sweet-faced dames,
  With all their trooping young,
Upraised their shining brows to heav'n,
  And sang as Israel sung:—

"Boom! iron-throated cannon, boom!
  Blow trumpets till ye crack!
Our way is forward up the hill
  And naught shall turn us back!"

Then Pleasure grasped the marshal fife,
  And Peace the war-like drum—
While every patriot cried, "To arms!
  Columbia has come!"

No lordly train her state disclosed,
  No golden crown or crest,
She came a daughter of the fields,
  A lily on her breast.

Yet born to crush the serpent's head—
  The simple cross she wore
First seen in Juda—freedom's sign—
  Stands firmest on our shore.

As beamed the star of Bethlehem
  Through centuries of strife,
So Liberty, the child of Love,
  Will live to gladden life.

And men will follow where she leads,
  O'er mountain, plain and sea,
Columbia upon their lips,
  Till all the world be free!

Till all the world, one brotherhood,
  Flame-purified of dross,
Each unto each is merciful
  As Christ upon the cross.

To Juda's Lord we bow the knee,
  The deeds of Greece we sing,
And to thy shores, O savage folk,
  The soul of both we bring!

Come thou and take this proffered flag,
  Reserved for him alone
Who holds his freedom dearer than
  A kingdom and a throne!

For where its blessed shadow falls
  Shall bloom the flower and vine,
And hand in hand through wood and field
  Our blood shall romp with thine,

While guns whose voices spoke of death
  Support the climbing rose,
And all the trophies of the war
  Beneath the cross repose.

ON GUARD IN LUZON

Slow back and forth with growing dread,
  My lonely round I pace.
The night is silent as the dead
  In some last resting place.

The sad-faced moon, low-hung, immense,
  Seems falling from the sky.
Afar the silent, ghostly tents
  In martial order lie.

Off shore, huge bulking on the tide,
  Gray ships of battle creep,
While fiery-eyed about them glide
  The dragons of the deep.

Strange whispers float from each retreat,
  At every sound I start,
And heavy-fingered moments beat
  A tattoo on my heart.

Where'er I look each object takes
  Some foreign shape and grows
Upon my vision till it breaks
  To twenty quickened foes.

With noiseless feet across my path
　　They leap to crouch and gibe,
Their goblin faces black with wrath,
　　An unknown, spectral tribe.

"Midnight! All's well!" The hollow cry
　　Sounds doleful as a knell;
"Post nine!" I hasten to reply,
　　"Midnight, and all is well."

To fight when cannon cheer the strife—
　　When steel to steel is laid—
To die red-soled with dews of life,
　　By worthy foeman's blade—

To flash one lingering look along
　　A ragged, charging line,
The last faint prayer a battle song—
　　Would such a death were mine!

But here to feel the sudden sting
　　Of coward's blade—to lie
A staring, crook'd, deserted thing—
　　God! what a death to die!

A night bird far within the wood
　　For sudden gladness sings;
"I fear not, for the Lord is good,"
　　Through all the silence rings.

And in that song I hear a prayer,
  Low, solemn, trusting, clear,
Of one who's doing picket there
  For me on picket here.

Still back and forth alone I pace,
  But went the hour I tell,
I see her pure, uplifted face,
  And know that all is well.

THE SINGER AND THE SONG

He wrote the song the soldiers sung;
   Poor, crippled and unknown.
They triumphed—how the heavens rung
When they came marching home and hung
Their trophies in the halls of state
And wore the favors of the great!—
   He died, unwept, alone.

'Twas come again, the sweet-toned day;
Again they stripped the trees of May
And came, close-buttoned to the chin,
Brave youth and vet'ran worn and thin,
To hall and park and post and grove,
While mother, wife, and sister wove
The lily, rose, and violet
And daffodil and mignonette
To garland fair and sweet bouquet
To deck the graves of blue and gray.

Again the fife call, loud and shrill,
Again the drumbeat, roll and trill,
Again the steady, rhythmic tramp
That once betokened field and camp,
Again the quick, commanding note,
Again the song the cripple wrote.

Mark where he sleeps—no shaft to grace
The sunken, bare, neglected place;
> But one who knew
> In passing threw
> His boutonniere upon the grave
And told a comrade. Down the line
It ran as runs along the shore
> A broken wave;
"My flowers for him!" "And mine!" "And mine!"
They cried. "Our country owes him more
Than all; his song inspired the deed."
And so till eve the blossoms fell
A fragrant shower. At last 'tis well.
And yet for him, poor bruised reed,
One act of kindness when he lay
In yonder bare, deserted room
Had changed his winter into May,
Had made his world to bloom.

Who knows? Mayhap the soul of him
> Who slept beneath that fragrant pile
Swept downward from some planet's rim,
Swept past the curved, barbaric moon,
> Soft thrumming on its harp the while,
Till, hovering o'er that sacred spot,
> It sang this new glad song of cheer,
> A song to North and South land dear,
A song that mothers love to croon,

As thus: God knows nor place nor lot,
His children all or far or near,
The Saxon and the cavalier,
  ·The rose-tree and forget-me-not.

THE ROCKY MOUNTAIN ANEMONE

(Written in the Garden of the Gods near Manitou, Colorado,
April 12, 1893.)

Sweet silver-stemmed anemone,
Fair delicate transparency,
Thy pale empurpled cup is filled
With nectar Hebe's trembling hand
From her now useless cup has spilled.
Poor Hebe, standing all aghast
Upon the sacred mountain side,
To see the gods contemptuous cast
    From throne magnificent,

        Swung wide
The gates, so long their grandeur kept
Close shut from eyes profane:

        The tide
Of progress to oblivion swept
Thy people, Manitou, and thou,
O Spirit Great, must shrinking flee
From cave to cave of thine own hills.
There's none so poor to name thee now—
That name, alas, has come to be
The sacrilegious sign of trade.
What wonder frighted Hebe spills
This nectar that I quaff from thee,
    Anemone, Anemone.

THE DREAMER

What part of me is this that goes
 Straight forth into the fields if I
But see the color of a rose
  Or hear a lonely sparrow cry?
    Neglectful of the task whose wage
    Scarce keeps me from a debtor's cage?

I know where you are stretched along
 The grassy border of a brook,
That dances to the robin's song
  Or laughs whene'er the cowslips look
    Into its depths to see, poor elves,
    A wrinkled semblance of themselves.

The fields are billowed like a sea—
 The robber wind your ready slave—
While you, contented as a bee,
  Half-drunken in his clover cave,
    List to the fife the crickets lip,
    And watch the honeysuckles trip.

The ants desert their toil for games,
 A holiday the songsters keep;
For you a cloudland city flames
  All gorgeous o'er the Western steep,
    And earth runs wildly, madly, free—
    Ah, God, the walls that compass me!

How shall my nest of waiting birds
  Be feathered from this barren brain?
What are to them the lowing herds
  And what the sunshine-flooded plain?
    Unsouled, I linger helpless here,
    With no companion but my fear.

Come back, come back, oh, truant soul!
  Come back to guide this idle pen;
The Juggernauts of commerce roll
  To crush the hopes of dreaming men.
    Without you, mine must perish so—
    Yet forth into the fields you go.

GARNERED TREASURES

Behold the garnered treasures of the field!
  All promises of April are fulfilled;
The earth exhausted with its bounteous yield,
  As some brown Samson suddenly o'er-willed,
    Shorn of its flowing locks all nerveless lies
    A hapless subject to the low'ring skies.

From distant fields come lowing herds of kine
  To lie at ease beside the bursting rick,
Content to know, with reason wond'rous fine,
  If, fast or slow, the clock of Nature tick,
    That shelter, food and drink in plenty wait
    To cheer their stay within the farmyard gate.

What though old Winter rouses in the north,
  Who fears him now that plenty reigns supreme?
The honest yeoman lead their children forth
  To mingle voices with the praiseful stream,
    The prayerful rushes and the chanting wood,
    In grand thanksgiving to the God of good.

Impatient Love, now weary tasks are done,
  Trips all as lightly to the homely tune
As fairies sporting where the brooklets run
  Through rose-trees nodding in the month of June.
    Hope long deferred a sweet fulfillment finds,
    As grapes give answer to the bending vines.

Not rural homes alone to-day are blest,
  The mother welcomes everywhere her child,
The worldling stands a sinner self-confessed
  And is again to Virtue reconciled.
    Thanksgiving for the spirit born of Thee,
    O man of God, in blessed Galilee!

From lowly vale and lofty mountain peak
  Still prayer and praise and glad thanksgiving rise;
The strong grow thoughtful of the poor and weak,
  The dove of peace from cot to palace flies,
    While strange, sweet music wakened by her wings
    Thrills every heart till every creature sings.

THE WEIGHT O' DISCONTENT

There's a heap o' foolish chatter, 'bout the way the
    world is run,
Men an' women allus tellin' o' the way it might be
    done,
But it seems to me the wisest jus' to let her roll an'
    siz,
Knowin' discontent is catchin' as the yeller fever is.

Carter hed a quarter-section that fur growin' crops was
    great,
Land was rich as all creation—warn't no better in the
    state.
Bill kep' workin' late an' airly—kep' the children at it
    too,
'Ceptin' when the school was runnin'—would ha' pulled
    the mortgage thro'.
If he'd had a mite o' backin', but his wife she couldn't
    see
Any future les'n famine—case in pint you must agree,
Fur Bill caught her discontentment—got discouraged,
    lost his grip,
An' the quarter-section dwindled to a twenty-acre strip.

Mercy Meredith's another—wuz as cheerful, peart an'
    spry
As 'n April-mornin' robin, or a flicker in July,
Father died an' left the humsted, house an' land an'
    all to her,

Every body said 'twuz proper; well she married Jacob
   Burr.
Proud an' selfish man wuz Jacob—holdin' gladness
   as a crime,
Kep' a naggin at her, preachin' meek submission all
   the time;
Jacob had no cause to blame her ef in time she turned
   to find
In some other voice the music that wuz singin' in her
   mind.
'Course she's got to bear the burden, but 'twas him that
   sewed the seed
O' the discontent that druv her to commit the wilful
   deed.

Where's the use o' seeking trouble? gladness dwells in
   everything.
Moles that burrow in the meadow, birds that mount
   an' sail an' sing,
Are the care o' Him that made 'em—they are happy one
   an' all—
While a man can leap the ditches he has no excuse to
   crawl;
You may ride a higher stepper than the gentle nag I
   own,
But my horse may still be joggin' when your handsome bay is blown.
Runnin' streams 'll tell a story jest as sweet to you
   or me
If we've tuned ourselves to hear it. All that's best in
   life is free.

Man may carry all o' Heaven 'thout his shoulders bein'
    bent,
But is crushed to earth with bearin' half a pint o' dis-
    content.
So it seems to me the wisest, jest to let the old world
    siz,
Knowin' discontent is catchin' as the yeller fever is.

OCTOBER

All day I have been in the woods alone,
  A day so quiet my soul could hear
The soul of the forest in pensive moan—
The soul of the forest in undertone,
  Bewailing the dying year.

In dim, soft shadow I roamed at will
  Where brooks, leaf-muffled and languid, flow.
So tensely tuned was the time, and still,
I could feel the heart of the forest thrill
  With the presage of coming woe.

I could feel the heart of the forest beat
  In sorrow at loss of its beautiful crown;
While up from the grasses an odor sweet—
A faint, sweet odor arose to meet
  The leaves that were drifting down.

The bright green leaves of the summer, alas!
  Now brown, and amber, and red, and gold—
I fell with my face in the dying mass,
For I felt the wings of a spirit pass,
  And the touch of a hand was cold—

The gruesome touch of a ghostly hand
   And the sigh of a soul's despair!
For the foes of Life were abroad in the land,
The wings of Destruction the forest fanned,
   And Beauty was dying there.

With my face in the crimson leaves I wept,
   (Dear leaves, so gay in the warm June weather!)
And into my bosom a longing crept,
That my soul with the soul of the leaves had kept
   On into the great Forever.

For dear to me was the Summer's bloom—
   But the world cares little to understand;
To-night I sit in my lonely room,
With my lonely life, in the deepening gloom,
   A withered leaf in my hand.

LOOKING UPWARD

Universal retrogression! coward phrase on perjured
    lips,
Burdening our song and story till distracted fancy
    trips
On the heels of revolution. Hath all pleasure taken
    wing?
Why delight in croaking ravens and neglect the birds
    that sing?
Why uproot the corn and lilies, sowing thistles in their
    stead,
To deplore the loss of beauty and bewail the lack of
    bread?
Come again, oh wise Athenian! Come again, oh gen-
    tle Pan!
Ere the mind is slave to muscle and creation miss the
    man.

Adam, seeking through an Eden, broke the twig he
    could not bend;
Eve, companion of perfection, rent the veil she could
    not mend,
Yet there always is a David for the giant's overthrow;
Science breaks the mass of substance—flesh is gross
    and all too slow

For this fearless age of progress; love will ever be the
  food
Of a Moses or a Lincoln. Hearts that win and cherish
  good—
Gentle hearts that scatter blessings, these perfect the
  Maker's plan,
Moving mind to conquer muscle ere the muscle con-
  quers man.

Dainty fingers weaving laces, sturdy hands that mine
  and mold,
Faith inspires them, duty guides them, or their tale is
  never told,
Or their task is never finished and the threads of silk
  or steel
Fall a weak and tangled pattern—reason vivifies the
  reel.
'Twas the heart and not the hammer changed the cabin
  to a home;
'Twas the soul and not the chisel carved the statue,
  shaped the dome;
Strongest beast may rule the jungle, swords obey a
  woman's fan;
Thus the breath of life is growing to its consummation
  —Man.

THE HERO OF THANKSGIVING

Far and away the swallows dip and rise,
 Among the last of Summer's devotees,
They write Regret across the Autumn skies
 Flecked all with white like inland running seas;
Deserted nests that cling the eaves along
 Are empty, but the ricks below are full—
The heart of man is glad to grateful song,
 For plenty makes his prospect beautiful.
    E'en the raggedy man,
      Napoleon,
    Who wags his beard at the clock,
      In this thankful time
      Sits down to dine
    With the stiff old Puritan stock.

The children come to feast abundant spread,
 Grown children with the silver in their hair,
And with them marked by hesitating tread
 And air subdued, their own dear offspring fare.
Afrighted still, till grandma's voice assures,
 And clouded skies begin at once to clear;
She to her own each fainting heart secures,
 And purifies with love the atmosphere;
    But the raggedy man,
      Napoleon,

A genius gone astray,
　　Through turkey thighs
　　Makes curious cries
Upon Thanksgiving day.

Before the feast what earnest prayers are said,
　　And at its close what heartfelt songs are sung,
Care and Regret to other scenes are fled
　　While words of kindness trip from every tongue.
The Graces bend to lift the mystic veil
　　That hides the future on all other days,
Where Plenty stands and Comfort cries "All hail!
　　Ye sons of men, join in the songs of praise!"
　　　　Then the raggedy man,
　　　　　Napoleon,
　　　　.Sits high in his humble seat,
　　　　　And he sings and he laughs,
　　　　　As he freely quaffs,
　　　　And he orders the dark o' the meat.

O rags that push the cup of Hope aside
　　At other times, your power is gone today;
The world has turned her back on selfish pride,
　　To do good deeds without the hope of pay;
So shall sweet sleep unwonted pillows bless
　　When western slopes have swallowed up the sun,

And for each act of special tenderness
  Unto the poor on this Thanksgiving done
      The raggedy man,
        Napoleon,
      Who lives like the sun or stream,
        Like the moon or rose
        With no thought of clothes
      Will bring you a blissful dream.

HAWAIIAN LOVE SONG

(The phrase upon which this poem turns is the most tender and eloquent expression of love and affection in the Hawaiian language.)

Our Northern tongue for battle,
    For argument and trade,
But not for wooing looks of love
    From eyes of doubting maid,
More sweet the story's uttered
    In far away Hawaii,
    Aloha nui loa
    Aloha nui oe.

The Dane, the Celt, the Saxon,
    Are lovers quite as true
As any e'er the tropic sun
    To dreamy roundness drew;
But none can voice so sweetly
    Love's glad triumphant joy,
As this untaught Hawaiian,
    Aloha nui oe.

Pale autumn pensive lingers
    Along the crimson wood,
Or bends to weep above the spot
    Where late the poppy stood,

And sighs as sighs the lover
  For one in far Hawaii,
    Aloha nui loa
    Aloha nui oe.

The mother rocking softly
  Her first-born, crooning low
The quaint, unwritten song of love
  That babes and mothers know.
Drifts where the palms are sighing,
  In far away Hawaii,
    Aloha nui loa
    Aloha nui oe.

Sweet phrase, all unacquainted
  With sound of care or strife,
Like love untutored come to speech
  You bubble into life!
O, dusky-eyed Koolele,
  O lithe-limbed blue-eyed boy,
    Aloha nui loa
    Aloha nui oe.

THE FORCE OF LOVE

Hold back thy whip, O master!
  Hold back thy curse and frown!
The demons of disaster
  Fear not the sword or gown;
The demons of disaster—
  They troop to wreck all ships—
Than winds of Heaven faster—
  Hold back thy frowns and whips.
    For these, the poor, thy brothers be—
    Remember Him of Galilee!

What other power can save thee
  From tempter drawing near?
From devils all that brave thee?
  His love alone they fear;
The devils all that brave thee
  What other is to stay?
Think on the love He gave thee;
  Love ever and alway.
    By sacrifice men come to bliss,
    There is no other path but this.

Behold the star that shineth
  Forever in the east!
Behold the rose that twineth
  Above the lair of beast!

Behold the rose that twineth
  To bless the monarch's bower,
The same His hand designeth
  To cheer the toiler's hour!
    The space between the poor and great
    His presence doth obliterate.

O perfect love that chideth
  The lightest thought of wrong!
O love that still abideth
  To make the weaker strong!
O love that still abideth
  When all else here hath fled,
Thou art! all safely rideth
  Thy barque the river dread.
    To make a lion of the dove,
    'Tis thine, O silent force of love.

RING IN THE NAZARENE

Born in a manger in Bethlehem,
  Thorny the path he trod,
Mournfully heavy the cross He bore,
  Heir to the wisdom of God.

Mournfully heavy the cross He bore,
  Broken and steep the way,
Dearer His message because of pain,
  Light of the world to-day.

Dearer His message because of pain,
  Like by its like caressed,
Gracious as rain to the sun-dried plain,
  Millions those tears have blest.

Gracious as rain to the sun-dried plain,
  Turning the dull earth bright,
Truth is in blossom because of Him,
  Ring in the Child of Light!

Truth is in blossom because of Him,
  Sin is grown old and gray,
Welcome the gladness of doing good,
  Welcome the gentler way.

Welcome the gladness of doing good,
  Welcome the joy of love,
Banish the serpent, the hawk and owl,
  Welcome the child and dove.

Banish the serpent, the hawk and owl,
  Banish the man-made creed,
Welcome the brotherhood broad, divine,
  Welcome the Man indeed.

Welcome the brotherhood broad, divine,
  Banish the narrow and mean,
So shall His kingdom be over the earth—
  Ring in the Nazarene!

SUN WORSHIPERS

The southwind whispered the slender grasses,
   Thank God for our prince, the sun,
The brooks that sang through the mountain passes
   Cried *Free by grace of the sun!*
And the bearded grain on the plain below
Bowed down to the dust in a fervent glow
   Of gratefulness to the sun.
The forest thrilled with a joy intense,
And the whole earth stirred with a gladsome sense
   Of thankfulness to the sun.

O hope of the earth and joy of the earth,
   However the clouds may run,
O health of the earth and wealth of the earth,
   O joy of the world, good sun!
So the wise men chant as they bow the head
When the grain is housed and the feast is spread—
   Ere the revelry is begun,
Ere song be sung or jest be spoken,
Ere salt be lipped or bread be broken,
   Thank God for our prince the sun.

THE PRINCE OF LIGHT

'Tis not the sun that rises in the east
  To light this joyous morn
But Christ himself the interceding Priest
  From sepulture new-born.

His glory all the vault of heaven illumes,
  Earth wakens to his smile,
The sacred flower the holy fane perfumes,
  Dome, altar, pew and aisle.

No grander sign the blessed God above
  To wayward man has given
Than Thou, our Brother, risen Lord of Love,
  Whereby to enter heaven.

Where'er we stray, whate'er our creed may be,
  What though we've worshiped Doubt
Throughout the year, today we worship Thee,
  And cast the Foul Fiend out.

The clear-voiced bells, keyed to a mellow tone,
  Are chiming far and near;
"Behold the angels roll the stone away,
  The Purified appear!"

Afar the Mount of Calvary looms along
　The sky, with crimson pied,
Upon it stands the Cross, erect and strong,
　Where Self was crucified.

But from its shade the spirit, Sacrifice,
　Moves peaceful and serene,
And thought by thought, mounts unto clearer skies
　Till, poised the worlds between,

She softly calls unto the fainting soul;
　"Thou wert not born to be
A dying thing.　Behold the destined goal
　Is Immortality!"

'Tis not the sun that rises in the East
　To glorify this day
But Christ himself, the interceding Priest,
　To lead and light the way.

AUERBACH'S EASTER

Dher year has blendy days vor vork,
  Und very few vor fun,
Like Yuly Fordt, ven effery phoy
  Is youst a vorking guhn;
Or Arbor day vhen all der town
  Is like von great big dhree,
Or Labor day, vhen not a man
  Vas kvite so big as me.
I like me dhoo Thanksgiving day
  Vhen gobble-turkeys fall,
But Christmas time my Yacob says
  Vas youst dher best of all.

Yorge Vashington he has his day,
  Vehm all dher bandts kom oudt;
St. Patrick, doo, ven Irishmens
  Dher shamrock vears aboudt,
But vhen my poys dher haymow climbs
  Und hens forget to lay,
I say undo Katrina dhen:
  Twas coming Easter day.

I learn me dot vhen milliner shop:
  Vas hiring plendy clerks

Und eggs vas getting high in price
  Dhere's not a hen vot vorks.
But vhen dher Easter morning comes
  Und vhile dher choirs sing,
Dose poys run in mit eggs enough
  To fill a circus ring:
Plue eggs, prown eggs, und red, und green,
  Dher like I neffer see,
"Dher hens vas laid dhem all lasdt night,"
  Dhey cry, und vinks by me.

Dot teaching of dher Christian church,
  Has saved dher vorld, I know,
Und idt vas beautiful to see
  Dher violet auf dher snow,
Dher Resurrection vot you call
  Dot makes der future sure,
I like dot ferry much myself
  Auf all der vorld vas pure.
I like to hear dose organs boom,
  Und peoples sing und sing,
Till all dher town vas like dher voods
  Of Schermany in Spring.
But ve must haf religions more
  To keep my poys away
F'om hen's nests all dher veek before
  Dot holy Easter day.

.

FISHIN'

Hungry fur a res'ful time?
Come t' Iowa an' climb
    Straddle ov a stranded log
'At a freshet's landed on
One o' them air san'bars in
Th' ole Wapsipinnicon.
    Minnie, grasshopper, er frog,
Arry one is good fur bait,
Then jest stretch yourself an' wait;
Reelin' in an' payin' out,
Birds a-chirpin' all about—
Meby get a sudden strike
From a silver-bellied pike,
Er a Anglo-Saxon bass,
Fightin' t' the very las'.
'Spose y' never see a fin,
'Spose y' never git a bite,
Thars th' clouds a driftin' white,
An' the pipin' plovers run
Down the san'bars in the sun;
An' the water croonin' sweet
Through th' willers at y're feet
While y' loll an' blink an' doze,
Wond'rin ef th' river flows
Right er left, er's standin' still,

Wond'rin' not enough to care,
Straddle uv th' basswood there.
Jes' you shake this roar an' fuss
Fur a week ur two with us.
Laziness 'll get her fill
Doin' nothin'—'thout a wish,
On'y jes' t' fish an' fish.
Iowa I'm talkin' on,
An' the Wapsipinnicon.

WHERE SHE USED TO BE

This is the blessed chamber where
    She used to be
Who made each hour of worldly care
    So glad to me;
Or near or far, while this one spot
    Her presence blest,
Fear or defeat I knew them not,
    But all was best.

So light the armor, yet so strong,
    Her fingers knit,
I rode triumphant over wrong
    Because of it.
Stripped, scourged, unhelped to onward fare—
    God pity me!
Alone within the chamber where
    She used to be.

THE TRAVELER'S NIGHT AT HOME

Gray twilight draws her curtains adown the windowed
    west,
Each object, shadow mantled, half seen is, half is
    guessed,
The stars o'erhead are blinking, as newly waked from
    sleep,
And drowsily regretting the vigil they must keep;
Sounds have a sharp distinctness the sun-hours never
    know,
And seem upon the senses to riper fullness grow,
While trembles through the valley, like thunder after
    rain,
The steady, solemn rumble of the near approaching
    train.

The over-crowded pavement, where lamps un-lidded
    glare,
Presents the old-time picture—Joy walking with
    Despair;
But where the suburbs nestle, beyond the city gates,
The people quiet gather about their cheerful grates
In neat and cosy parlors which breathe a restful air
That wakes the heart to rapture is felt no other where.
Ah! fortune-favored mortals, with never need to roam,
You may not know how fondly the traveler loves his
    home.

The wife is tripping, tripping with anxious, thoughtful
    haste,
To see the many knick-knacks in pleasing order
    placed;
Here dressing-gown and slippers rest, with inviting
    look,
Beside the favored arm-chair rolled into pleasant nook
Before the polished hearth-stone—the foot-stool ready
    stands—
The very air seems softened by touch of loving hands,
And mother-eyes are beaming with an expectant light
Which says, "O time the sweetest, my traveler comes
    tonight!"

Within the curtained window his cherished offspring
    twain,
Their eager, hopeful faces close pressed against the
    pane,
Peer out into the darkness, their swelling hearts abeat
With keen anticipation, each anxious first to greet
The music of his foot-fall—At once he's at the door,
And joyful cries are ringing, while kisses by the score
His bearded face o'ershower as he enclasps their
    forms
And lifts them to his bosom with strong but gentle
    arms.

She, shunning demonstration, which oft proclaims
    deceit,
Her eyes like melting jewels, gives welcome true and
    sweet,

Takes down the clinging children, his wrappings lays
    aside,
Then modestly precedes him, with pardonable pride,
To where his comforts wait him—beguiles him of his
    trip—
Removes the laid-off garments, sets by the "battered
    grip,"
Till ere he scarce perceives it, so deft and dextrous
    she,
He's slippered, gowned and seated, a child upon each
    knee.

With merry word she leaves them, by household duties
    pressed;
The curly heads confidingly are pillowed on his breast;
Their silken tresses stroking, transfigured in the grate,
He sees his darlings growing to man and maid's
    estate;
The mystic veil is lifted that hides the future years,
And on his pensive vision a fair To Be appears.
Swift up the Mount of Progress advancing they are
    seen.
And white-browed Honor leads them and Virtue walks
    between.

About the table gathered, each lowly bows the head,
While humbly and devoutly the homely grace is said;
No long-drawn invocation to tire the Throne of Grace,
Nor abject self-abasement with pride writ on its face;
But praise and service tendered for life and health
    preserved;

This plain thanksgiving over, the waiting meal is
    served;
No feast, however costly, by lords and ladies shared,
E'er gave more grateful pleasure than this by love pre-
    pared.

The little heads are nodding, the bright eyes strive in
    vain
To look "I am not sleepy" yet close and close again,
Till sweet goodnights are given and mamma leads
    away.
But drifting down the stillness, he hears his Robbie
    say,
"Forever and Forever," then halt before amen—
"Dear Jesus don't let papa go away from us again."
His face is calm and tranquil again she has appeared,
But she can note the diamonds that glisten in his
    beard.

Their eyes have sudden meeting, no need for further
    speech,
She nestles close beside him, each takes the hand of
    each,
Against his rugged shoulder, she lays her golden
    tresses,
And they are lost in dreaming of timid, first caresses,
When she, a bashful maiden and he, an awkward
    youth—
She glances shyly upward, both catch the pleasant
    truth

And laugh in pleasant chorus—but still the faint per-
    fume
Of dewy summer evening seems floating through the
    room.

God's blessing on the fireside, whatever lot surrounds,
That to the holy music of wedlock still resounds!
Where confidence unbounded and love communion
    hold,
Where children's voices mingle;—let misers hoard
    their gold,
Ambitious statesmen wrangle; within this hallowed
    light
Dissension never wanders and greed can never blight.
Oh! picture all the raptures beneath yon starry dome,
The holiest are clustered around the Night at Home.

JUST OVER THE HILL

Just over the hill is the river of Peace
  In the valley of Sweet Content,
Where sins will perish and joys increase
  Till the whole vast firmament
Is white as the bosom of lily-bells,
  With the Christ-pure thoughts that rise
To the guardian soul of the world, who dwells
  In the garden of Paradise.

The world will be singing with softest tone
  In the love-land yet to be;
And flowers will bloom from the seeds once sown,
  In the beautiful Galilee.
'Twas the brook that told me this hopeful tale,
  And the wind with a voice of cheer
Cried; Patience, for there is no echoing wail
  Of the sorrows that haunt you here!

The skies will be brighter in time to come,
  The feet will have smoother way,
And follow a mellower fife and drum
  Straight into the Christ-made day.
I hear these words at the noon of night,
  When the clock and my heart are one,
And the wearisome burdens grow strangely light
  Ere the birth of the new-day sun.

Then I welcome the troubles that erst depressed,
  And cheerfully toil in my place,
For I know the sunbeams at birth caressed
  The hail that beats in my face.
I know that oppression is only a cloud
  Which faith may banish at will,
 And the straight shall be those whom today has
    bowed
  In the valley just over the hill.

WHEN LOVE IS QUEEN

Upon a cliff above the sea
That wooes the shore unceasingly
Love wanders to and fro.
A crown of light her brow adorns,
But on her breast a cross of thorns,
The while in accents low and sweet
She chants: When eve and morning meet,
When earth and sea and sky are one,
As free as sunbeams to the sun,
As free as winds that kiss the trees,
To all the worlds and stars of these
      My own shall come and go.
When love is queen—not love that blinds,
But constant love that seeks and finds
To keep till all the years are white
As lily lips that kiss the night—
Then hearts will woo as roses woo,
And souls will love as lilies do,
In that bright, glad, eternal day
When man nor world can say her nay.

FIRST OF THE SEASON

Winds er gettin' sort o' snappy,
  Clouds er mixin' brown an' gray,
Kind o' signs et makes me happy—
  I'm a-waitin' fur th' day
When there'll be a soun' like sighin'
  In the trees about the town—
Fun ov all kinds will be flyin',
  When the snow is comin' down.

Mandy says her time o' year is
  Buddin', leafin', growin' spring,
When in every sound you hear is
  Somethin' sweet an' promising—
She's a girl and girls are silly,
  Spec'ly when there's boys aroun'—
Give me winter, sled, an' Billy,
  An' the snow a-coming' down.

Mother's fond o' June and roses,
  Says they're company fur her,
Talks to all the plants and poisies—
  Wonder what she does it fur.
Don't I like 'em—well, I may sir,
  Jes coz mother does—Ge ho!
Whoop, go long! This is my day, sir.
  Jemenetty, see her snow!

AMBER

A strength sublime, a soul so rare
    She moved alone;
So have I seen a lily flare,
    Above its zone,—
A tiger lily, bravely bent
    Against the wind;
Its colors all from heaven lent,
    Superb, refined
By natures alchemy of tears,
    Rebuffs and shocks;
Free as the sun of doubts and fears,
    It patient rocks
Above the croaking multitude
    That gnaw below;
Amidst a throng in solitude,
    Yet all aglow
With warmth and color—
    Helpful sign
Still unto me,
    I see the tiger lily shine
And it is thee.

SANTA CLAUS

You'd teach my little Jamie that there ain't no Santa
    Claus?
Don't doubt it, Parson Bradford. We must stare, and
    doubt, and pause,
While stars in grand procession chant continuous to
    the Lord,
While Ocean feeds the marshes in obedience to his
    word!
But tides and stars are nothing more, in God's eternal
    plan,
Than Santa Claus of Christmas to that chubby little
    man.
Far better strike the beauty from the Spring for you
    and me
Than kill the ancient Spirit of the children's Christ-
    mas tree.

You've studied Taine and Tyndall, Kant and Darwin,
    I'll allow;
I'm satisfied to follow just the Bible and the plow;
To sow and garner; learn the ways of insect, bird, and
    beast,
To love the robin's treble when the dawn comes up
    the East,
A song as sweet and soulful as the dear old-fashioned
    rhymes

That mother sings at evening. You forget the glowing
times
When we hung our home-knit stockings, with a faith
that naught could shake,
In the wide, smoke-painted chimney; when we lay for
hours awake,
Hoping still to hear the footfall of the reindeer in the
snow!
Do you think I'd rob my Jamie of the joys I used to
know?

There's one thing greater, Parson, than a scientific
truth,
'Tis to keep the old heart gentle with the memories of
youth.
Love is God, and shines eternal, making rainbows in
our tears;
Day to Night is elder brother through the stately step-
ping years;
You would crush the faith that triumphs in the awful
strife with death;
You would banish Burns and Shakespeare and the
Man of Nazareth.
You're a parson, I'm a toiler, but, by all the sacred
past,
I will beat the plowshare narrow for the curs't icono-
clast.

FARMER BUNNER

Farmer Bunner, big and homely,
  Rich in land but poor in speech;
Kittie Brown, petite and comely,
  Pretty as a blushing peach,
Said by all her friends to be
Worthy mate of high degree.

Not that she was so aspiring;
  Beauty didn't make her proud,
Rather bashful and retiring;
  Still the neighborhood allowed
That the man for Kittie Brown
Was some cavalier from town.

Then it was the homely Bunner
  Seemed to fill her modest eye,
Seeing which he wooed and won her—
  Now the other maidens cry
To their mother's, nodding grim,
"She wa'nt good enough for him!"

BLESSINGS THAT COME UNAWARES

We thank Thee, O Father of Mercy,
  For the blessings that come unawares,
Well knowing what's won by pursuing
  But adds to the sum of our cares.

From morning to morning we labor,
  The task we would do is not done,
And the things that seem great in the distance
  Are nothing when once they are won.

No one thing is worthy of worship,
  And all things when clasped in the hand
Are naught but the signs of the music;
  The symphony only is grand.

The manna that falls in the desert,
  The dry, dusty desert of strife,
Is sweeter than fruit to whose growing
  We've given the years of our life.

The bud that escapes us while searching
  The bush for its promise so sweet
Goes straight to the heart with its blooming,
  And the instant is all but complete.

In vain through the volumes of wisdom
  We seek for the blissful, and lo!
The soft lisping accents of childhood
  Set all of God's kingdom aglow.

The joy is in building the temple,
  The substance is less than the dream,
And the song that we sing but the echo
  Of the perfect one heard in the stream.

Those things that are won by pursuing
  But add to the sum of our cares;
We thank Thee, O Father of Mercy,
  For the blessings that come unawares.

THE TRUE AMERICAN

America! Inspiring theme!
  Immortal goddess crowned
With jewels brought from every stream
  To shine the world around.

'Gainst foreign foe thy sturdy sons
  Have never known defeat;
And North and South, behold their guns
  Stacked at the Nation's feet!

Thy eldest, born at Bunker Hill,
  With flowing locks of gray
Stood stern beside the youth of will
  At Sàntiago bay.

"Fourth of July!" out o'er the main
  The Union liners roared,
"For liberty make way!" again
  The song to heaven soared.

Swift onward to the farthest shore
  The grateful message ran,
While all the world bowed low before
  The true American.

"I fight to free my brother brave,"
  Said Washington, "And I,
To free my brother who is slave,"
  Was Lincoln's loftier cry.

But loftier still from Cuban coast
  The blessed challenge rose:
"We fight that strangers may be free,
  All tyrants are our foes!"

And onward still to every clime,
  Where'er a river runs
That oars may sweep in martial time,
  Shall go our men and guns,

While over them shall break and float
  The banner of the free,
Till all the sons of earth shall vote
  It full supremacy.

Then shall the heaven-born symbol hold
  No hint of tear or sigh,
But only God's great promise told
  To man from Sinai.

GETHSEMENEA

Like fog-bound ships we blindly grope
  An unknown way. But God is good,
And multiplies the lamps of hope,
  And knits the strands of brotherhood.
·Behold across the darkened wave,
  Gethsemenea's enduring ray!
And men are manning boats to save,
  Who were adrift but yesterday.

THE UNIVERSAL UNION

Join the union? Won't accept me; I'm a capit'list, you
    see.
Hear that voice? That's mother singing. See this
    youngster on my knee?
Half a dozen others romping just outside there in the
    snow;
ˆI'm a Croesus—shut the door, you—what's the trouble,
    Jack? Hello!
Broke a runner? Bess, the tweezers—good as new, eh?
    Price? a kiss.
Coasting sir's a healthy pleasure, one that older people
    miss.
Union? Yes, I favor unions, but the one I advocate
Must establish helpful kindness and abolish hurtful
    hate.

Rented? No, the place is mine, sir. House and little
    patch o' ground,
That the children work in summer—fruit is sweeter, I
    have found,
When the trees and vines that bear it are the product
    of our care,
And the flowers the wife has tended are a hundred
    times more fair
For the gentle touch o' fingers guided by a heart that
    loves 'em,

And their colors are the richer for the face that's bent
    above 'em.
I'm in favor of the union, but I'm very free to state
That the union of the fireside is the one I advocate.

If my neighbor has a carriage he must keep a coach-
    man, too,
And they're often lots· of trouble. What we are, not
    what we do,
Makes us rich; the simple toiler, loved and loving wife
    and child,
Is among the richest living. What is golden treasure
    piled
In the vaults of all the nations when you stand beside
    the bed
Of the darling you have worshiped and they tell you
    "She is dead?"
There are bonds that reach to heaven, and this bit of
    silken hair
Kept between the Bible covers forms a union here and
    there.

Troubles come to everybody; strength in numbers, I'll
    agree;
But the union of the babies and the wife's enough for
    me.
We'll continue on together, keeping this one point in
    view:
"What I wish" is not the question, but "What can I do
    for you?"

Were this humble cot a palace and this meager bit of
  ground
Wide as all the state o' Texas, 'twould be only farther
  round;
Drawing near to helpful kindness, keeping far from
  hurtful hate,
Holding fast to those that love you, make the creed I
  advocate.

THE RIVER OF LOVE

If Faith and Hope and Charity wait
The word of the Master to open the gate
That the river of love may flow—
Dear Lord, let the word be said,
That the River of Love may thread
  And leap and tumble
  Where homes are humble,
  May plead and chide
  By the hall of pride,
And croon and droon where the weary keep
Wide-eyed and wan and know not sleep—
  Ere the waiting die,
  And the halting cry
  "Too late! too late!
  We knock at the gate
  Without reply!"—
  O Thou Most High,—
The brown wood kneels by the sin-dry bed
Of the River of Love! Let the word be said.

———

Then the Master signaled the Sisters Three,
 Who were holding the love-gate fast,
And they slipped the bar and they turned the
  key,
 And the River of Love rolled past—

Rolled on to freshen the withered wood,
Rolled on to nourish the kind and good,
　Which the angels sang to see.
O the sands leaped up to the river's swell,
The great rocks trembled—the sin-walls fell,
And devils went wailing about in hell
　Because that the good should be.
And the Sisters Three, by the gate above,
Cast flowers to drift on the River of Love.

AUERBACH'S BABY

You haf not seen him? Ach, mein herr,
Besser you lose you zwanzig year
Your life oud aber miss dot dear,
    Das kleine kind, my baby.

Vhen vitsles blow by efening time
Und I fon vork come kvick zu heim,
Eef you could see him creep to climb
    My knees oup—dot schmall baby!

His fingers auf mine eye he stdicks,
He rumps mine hair und crows und kicks,
Und plays a hundred funny dricks
    Like dot, my leedle baby.

On kaltes night bout dhree o'clock
He dries to vake oudt half dher block,
Und I must valk und valk und valk
    Mit dot schmall rascal baby.

I sing him auf dot lulaby
Undill my dhroad vas cracking dhry,
Und coax him dot he close his eye
    Und go to sleep, my baby.

Dhen roundt my neck he makes his arm,
So schubby, dimpled, soft und varm—
O, may dhere neffer come some harm
  To dot schmall, leedle baby!

SPRING

The south wind caught two sunbeams
  'Mong orange blooms at play,
And over mountains bore them
  To where the snowdrifts lay.
In soft, warm arms it bore them
  To far off Northern land
Where brooks were bound in fetters
  Wrought by the ice king's hand,
Till by an ancient maple
  The south wind set them free,
    And the sunbeams smiled
    Where the snow was piled,
  And danced in the leafless tree.

The snow drift moved and melted,
  The brook its shackles cast,
And through the ancient maple
  The sap ran free and fast;
The cold earth stirred and murmured,
  A violet brave looked up,
And the sunbeams came from the branches
  And hid in its purple cup.

A POEM

Of God-like wisdom a tuneful sage
Wrote Life's full song on a single page;
It was good to hear—
It swung in the ear,
  It rung in the soul
Till the days were thrilled,
Till the years were filled
  With its measured roll.

All seasons marched in the swelling lines;
It sobbed as the wind in the needled pines,
It held the motion of meadow grass
When troops of the dimpled fairies pass
And the rhythmic beat of the rose that creeps
To the moonlit room where my lady sleeps.
'Twas a grand, sweet song and a Soul of Light
Came out of the sky on an Autumn night
To bear it away to that world afar
Where Truth holds court in a flaming star.
"It is good" said Truth, "but the song I crave
Will never be written I fear, O slave!"
Again he searched through the earth below,
And brought her a flake of the new-born snow,
Then Truth devoutly bowed low her head,
"You have found a poem at last," she said.

E-O-EAVE

Ever notice et a raisin'
　　When the pikes are in the bent
Et the man who grunts the loudest
　　Alus is, by accident,
On the eend that lags 'n lingers,
　　But at soun' uv dinner-horn
Ez the spryes' 'n the quickes'
　　Man et ever could be born.

Larn a heap frum bees 'n raisin's
　　Ef ye never seed a book,
"E-O-Eave" won't lift a scantlin'
　　But it hustles up the cook.
Watch the man et keeps a liftin',
　　Still ov lip an' set ov chin,
An' you'll see him on the ridge-pole
　　When it's time t' drive the pin.

WAITING

Still in a cove my pinnace lies
    With ready oar;
Above it smiles propitious skies,
    Afar before
The quick-winged swallows dip and rise
    And dart and soar,
Inviting action, yet I wait,
Nor care to venture my estate.

Out to the rythmic, rocking sea
    My bark will float,
When one grand song that lives in me,
    Unformed, remote,
Shall stir the land to ecstasy
    By its full note—
Shall thrill the sands to sing again
And challenge Ocean—not till then.

A SEASON OF PEACE

March trumpets and the violet
  Springs up to cheer the wood;
E'en so' when storms of Winter fret,
Does Christmas bloom lest we forget
  The joy of doing good.

Sweet day, when every bosom thrills
  With such a joy as stirr'd
The Wise Men when, above the hills,
They saw the Star whose glory fills
  And beautifies the Word.

Now soldiers leave the field of strife,
  And battle flags are furled,
While in the marts where trade was rife
There moves a mercy-loving life,
  A charitable world.

Sweet favors bloom in all that's said,
  No selfish acts oppress,
But joys return we've counted dead—
He maketh smooth the path we tread
  With special tenderness.

O bells of golden gladness, ring!
  The stream of plenty flows,
The world hath gifts to surfeiting,
Today our brother Christ is King
  And rules the hearts He knows.

THE BLACKBIRD

There's a tuneful blackbird sitting in a balmy mountain
     pine,
  And his shadow to my window by the orient sun is
       cast,
Where it dances on the curtain in an ever-changing
     line,
   While the musical magician summons visions of the
        past.
Oh, the days when I was happy and as innocent as he
Who thrills me with his "tonkle, tinkle, tonkle, pip,
     g-e-e!"

Out upon you, masquerading in a sober, priestly coat
   While you're gay as any lover when his Jean is
       passing kind!
And you spill such wealth of gladness from your palpi-
       tating throat
    That I feel its blissful pulsing in the channels of the
        wind,
While the cares of life are drifting farther, farther out
     to sea—
'Tis the king of all magicians calling to me from the
     tree.

Now the lady-slippers tangle with the honeysuckle
     vines
   Where the brook above the pebbles sings the tune-
       fulest of tunes;

Now the redbud's in its glory and the pollard willow
    shines,
  And the piping plovers gather on the damp and bar-
    ren dunes;
For the days of love and laughter, love and laughter
    sweet and free,
Come again to cheer the lonely with the blackbird in
    the tree.

NO DEATH FOR HEROES

The firemen who were victims of the cold-storage fire, in
the World's Fair grounds, were buried in one grave, and the
floral offerings placed on the mound in memory of their dar-
ing entirely hid the mounds from view.

Christ lives. His gentle spirit
  O'erleaps the snares of vice
To sow life's tangled pathways
  With seeds of sacrifice.

And streams of mercy follow
  Where'er those feet have trod,
Till every sob of sorrow
  Breaks at the feet of God.

Where sand-dunes drank the lifeblood
  Of Christian's far advance,
Behold a perfect city
  Mock tomahawk and lance.

And peristyle and palace
  And emerald-banked lagoon
Show in the sunless midnight
  As brightly as at noon.

There heaps a world its treasure,
  The best from everywhere—
The city sacrificial,
  Mankind's white altar-stair.

An altar-stair of wisdom
  Where nations mount apace
To merciful communion
  And brotherhood of race.

O wonderful dream city
  To wither in a breath!
But no, these souls heroic
  For thee go down to death.

So from some sudden impulse
  Springs every thought of worth,
So in some heartfelt action
  World-wonders all have birth.

The poorest flower that nestles
  In yonder wreath of fame
Found life 'midst battling forces
  And bloomed—a child of flame.

Thus names the world holds lightly
  In some great stress of strife
Wake suddenly to beauty
  And everlasting life.

There is no death for heroes;
  Their souls move on sublime
To set the lamp of progress
  On shores unknown to time.

Behold! These lowly houses
   We deck with bloom today
Are empty all—Christ Jesus
   Hath rolled the stone away.

And far beyond our knowing,
   Where creeds will not suffice,
They march among the honored,
   God's own through sacrifice.

PLEA FOR THE FLOWERS.

Shall all these flow'rs be sacrificed
  On Decoration day?
The lily was far more to Christ
  Than Solomon's array;
Our nation's dead, where'er they tread,
  Must cry: "Let live the rose;
Let live the pansy in its bed;
Slay not—there is no hero dead—
  Slay not a flow'r that grows!"

Give songs that ripple over words
  Like brooks o'er pebbled sands,
As glad as are the hymns of birds
  In sunny southern lands.
Give thoughts that thrill, but do not kill,
  Give lessons broad and grand,
Hug to thy bosom "Peace be still"—
Strip not the fragrant wood and hill
  With desecrating hand.

Heap all these graves of precious mold
  With deeds of love and cheer;
And make the day a thread of gold
  To mark the graying year.
Be thy soul's food a comrade's good,
  Thy strife to banish pain;
The day is hardly understood—
No violet in yonder wood
  Should mourn her children slain.

PRAYER FOR KIPLING WHEN HE LAY AT THE POINT OF DEATH

"The road to Mandalay" is drenched
  With tears we cannot stay;
With "Gunga Din" we pray to win
  Respite for him today.

At last "there's neither east nor west,"
  The world is clasping hands
In silent prayer for him, the great
  Exemplar of all lands.

Take up the brave man's burden, Lord!
  Let pass this bitter cup;
"He trod the ling like buck in spring,"
  Hold Thou his spirit up!

The tinkling of the tambourine,
  The bugle's lilting notes,
The roar of guns, the beat of steam,
  Are tugging in our throats.

The onward march of purpose high,
  The sail of gracious power,
The surging, swelling, lifting song,
  Come back to fill the hour.

And trumpet-tongued they plead with Thee
  To stay the awful blow,
At last "there's neither East nor West."
  And he hath made it so.

THANKSGIVING AT THE HOMESTEAD

Frost has crimsoned all the leaves,
But the barn is rich in sheaves,
Ricks of clover scent the air,
Fruits await the housewife's care,
Haws are black above the rills,
Kine are sleek upon the hills,
And along the orchard wall
Pipes the quail his cheerful call.

Fast beside the glowing grate
(Locks as white as ocean foam!)
Now the aged couple wait
For "the children" coming home—
Children who from far and near
At Thanksgiving gather here;
Children bowed with toil and care,
Girls with silver in their hair,
Boys with beards like harvest grain,
All "the children" come again,
Mingling golden locks with gray
On this peaceful, prayerful day.

Here the oaken table waits,
Set with two long rows of plates
That no Curlyhead may pout
Lest the grown folks crowd him out.
Even roving, wayward Tim

Finds a place reserved for him,
And ere grandpa's prayer is done
Vows a better course to run.
Banished every doubt and fear
From this hopeful atmosphere.

Blest the visions that arise!
Grandpa looks in grandma's eyes.
Griefs that furrowed cheek and brow,
Tears and sighs forgotten now.
Only sunshine floods the way
Looking backward from today.

"Thou who rulest everywhere,
Be our children still Thy care,
On the sea or on the land
Keep them ever in Thy hand,
Guiding still in rain or sun,
May Thy love still make us one
And its sweetness ne'er depart
From the homestead of the heart."

This the father's earnest prayer,
And "the children" gathered there
Feel renewed the hopes of youth
Flame again with love of truth,
And new armored for the fray
Bless again Thanksgiving day.

THE SOUL OF OLD GLORY

With drum and fife and bristling blade
  The columned lines, in steady tread,
Sweep broadly down the streets of trade,
  Old glory flying overhead,
  And not a man to freedom bred
But draws a fuller, deeper breath,
To see our glorious shibboleth.

O'er desert sands, far out at sea,
  Where icebergs lift, by dusky isles,
Yon starry emblem of the free
  Above the babel-haunted smiles,
  And, spite of kings' or courtiers' wiles,
The meek leap up to rule as when
The Savior called—and slaves are men.

Not all the darkness of the world
  Can hide your light, oh, stars that shine
From folds that never will be furled
  While beauty loves a swelling line;
  Thou art Jehovah's latest sign
Set in the atmosphere of earth,
Assuring final power to worth.

MY ROBBIE

I know the sun is shining, but alas! I cannot see!
I know the birds are singing in every bush and tree,
But there's neither light nor music in the world for
    me—
    My Robbie fell in front at Santiago.

They say the starving Cubans at last are being fed,
They say the haughty Spaniards before our forces fled,
And that our country's glory to the farthest land has
    spread,
    But Robbie fell in front at Santiago.

O Queen of cruel subjects! O Queen of cruel smiles!
What are your ships and treasure, your sunny South-
    ern isles?
Take them back and give his mother, from the dark
    defiles,
    Her boy who fell in front at Santiago.

UNDER THE CYPRESS

Beside the river dark and deep—
  The curls a-cluster round her face—
  She lieth, as from Pleasure's chase
O'erwearied, sunk to sudden sleep.

The somber cypress bows above,
  Wherein the gentle Zephyr seem
  To chant, accordant with the stream,
A requiem o'er the death of Love.

The waters creep so carefully
  Among the shells and pebbled sands,
  And steal to touch her waxen hands—
Dear hands are clasped so prayerfully.

What sweet simplicity of dress—
  Nor is there guile in this pure face,
  But only faith and gentle grace.
And loving trust and tenderness.

A barque so frail—O fateful praise!—
  Life's sea should ne'er have ventured o'er,
  But kept its course along the shore,
In sheltered nooks of quiet bays.

These simple lines tell all we know:
"O God, forgive the wicked work!
I may not sleep behind the kirk,
But lay me where the daisies grow.

"Where sunbeams in the grasses lurk,
Where violets are first in bloom,
I may not lie in hallowed tomb—
'Tis holy ground behind the kirk."

What marvel that this calm retreat
Unwontedly her thought should woo,
It was the only path she knew
Led out to solitude complete.

Sad, staring eyes that seem to wait
The coming of this closing touch—
She loved, and, loving overmuch,
Some hearth, some home is desolate.

TACITA

The eye that flasheth worldly pride,
　The lip that frameth worldly scorn,
Are servants to a cruel heart
　That better never had been born.

Where Peace is queen the soul impels
　A softly radiant, constant beam,
That falls upon the fretful world
　Like moonlight on a turbid stream.

Tacita, bend thy gaze on me,
　Unveil those almond orbs of thine,
And let the moonlight of thy soul
　Into my troubled bosom shine.

Then, though the night of Care surround,
　Inspired by thee, my voice I'll rear
And wake the silence to a song
　The vagrant winds shall hush to hear.

MISMATED

"Good-night," I cried; they tossed me back good-
  byes.
  (What is a year?   A dead leaf in a flame),
So quickly back and forth Time's shuttle flies,
  'Tis gone ere we have thought the word to frame.

I see them now close standing side by side—
  He tall and strong, with eyes of Saxon blue;
She lithe and slender, dark and dreamy-eyed,
  A blushing rosebud freshed with morning dew.

She clinging as the climbing rosebush clings;
  He like an oak that braves the wintry blast;
She warm and pulsing as the thrush that sings;
  He calm and cold—a Viking of the past.

O heartless love, to bind the northern pine
  And southland rose within your magic link;
The mountain torrent and the lowland wine,
  The crag-bred eagle and the bobolink.

The year is past. I come again tonight,
  Impatient-footed.   Not a welcome breath;
The tropic's fervor loosed the snowy height
  That, avalanching, bore them both to death.

LOVE'S TELLING

I love thee. The blood of my being
  Seems all to be flooding my heart; .
As the poor, hunted hare in the hedge-row,
  At the sound of each accent I start—
Start forth but to shrink from the sunlight,
  And creep back again to the shade,
Afraid of the stir in the grasses
  My own timid movements have made.

O tongue, a most eloquent pleader
  Art thou when I muse on her name!
Drawn near her; my thoughts are as ashes
  Of words consumed in love's flame.
Alone, sweetest phrases and glowing
  Are born of my being's desire.
With her, I have nothing but silence—
  The heart in my bosom on fire.

O rose. for thy passionate language!
  O brook, for they musical tones!
My heart is o'erburdened with love-words,
  For speech I have nothing but moans.
I will cast off the spell that enchains me—
  All the wealth of my passion I'll pour
At her feet—O, I love thee! I love thee!
  I love thee! Ah can I say more?

VICTOR HUGO

O Master of the earth's divine,
  Thy genius flushed our sky so bright
That countless souls yet strong in thine
  Press upward toward the purer light;
Stern-featured, thou wert quick as Christ
  To weep for griefs by others borne,
And, ever from thyself enticed,
  Mourned that the world had cause to mourn.

Two million feet with solemn tread
  Beat out thy dirge in funeral train,
But twice ten million hearts, O dead
  Yet living Hugo, join the strain;
So long as right to might must kneel,
  Or while there lives one fettered slave,
Or slaves go free, or freedmen feel—
  So long shall tears bedew thy grave.

THE PANSY

Three flowers in my garden grew;
  A lily, pansy, and a rose.
I questioned Psyche: "Tell me true,
  Which is most beautiful of those?"

The lily, hearing, reared its head.
  "Behold the charm of grace," it cried.
"Voluptuous beauty here is bred,"
  The blushing rose as quick replied.

The pansy, drooping on its stem,
  Concealed its face with modest start
"Alas!" I said, "pride ruins them"—
  I wear the pansy in my heart.

WHEN BESSIE COMES DOWN TO THE SPRING

The daisies nod merrily one to the other,
  The marigolds cling to the hem of her gown,
The chickens desert their excitable mother,
  To clamor for favors, when Bessie comes down
With her pail to the spring. Oh, red and white roses,
  Not fairer are they, all a-bloom in the grass,
Than the bloom of her cheek—see how graceful she
      poses,
  To watch the cloud shadows that lazily pass;
And birds linger, praiseful, on fluttering wing,
When hazel-eyed Bessie comes down to the spring.

The rabbit peeps shyly from under his cover
  Of thick-blossomed lilac adorning the slope,
To gaze with the eloquent eyes of a lover
  Where Bessie is tripping, like radiant Hope
From the dream of a poet; her free flowing tresses
  By arrows of sunlight pierced many times through–
And Brindle comes lowing to meet her caresses;
  The grass showing dark where she scatters the dew—
While backward and forward complacently swing
The minnows, when Bessie comes down to the spring.

Her charms owe no tax to the cold law of fashion,
  She had all her grace from the glorified One;
And her veins are as free of the latter-day passion

As meadow-stream kissed by the beams of the sun.
No fairies beguile her—poor waifs of the attic—
  In operas fashioned to mountebank's art,
But she hears the lark's melody ripple ecstatic
  And full from his throat, whereon lieth his heart;
While up through the clover with giant-like swing,
Comes Reuben to welcome sweet Bess at the spring.

LOVE'S ORACLES

Above the hills the Orient sun
  Peeped through a mist of gold,
That downward from his ardent gaze
  Into the valley rolled;
And fleeing Night, with jealous hand,
  Plucked from the changing skies
Two sister stars, and refuge sought
  Within my lady's eyes.

That home once gained, she ne'er forsook—
  Why leave a place so fair?
But set the stars, as lamps of love,
  To light the darkness there.
Now I, to know how fickle Chance
  Her favors may bestow,
In faith, consult those heavenly orbs
  That 'neath her eyelids glow.

SWEET, BEAUTIFUL EYES

Sweet, beautiful eyes! Soft, beautiful eyes!
So tenderly, tranquilly, soulfully wise!
In their fathomless depths such beauty I see
That I bow the head and I bend the knee
In humble worship. O, love divine!
Unselfish affection; I see it shine
In those eloquent orbs. O land! O sea!
  O limitless azure! O star gem'd skies!
Of all known treasures not one to me
  So dear as the light of my lady's eyes.

O limpid, liquid, glorious eyes!
What care I for time, if it stays or flies,
When my life is lit by those radiant beams?
The work-a-day world with its sordid schemes,
It is nothing to me, for I live and move
In a separate, rhythmical realm of love.
The creeds of the earth they are nothing to me—
  My altar, cathedral, my heaven is there;
And I bow the head and I bend the knee
  To worship the eyes of my lady fair.

THE BITTER-SWEET VINE

She came in the dawn of a sweet May morn,
  Laden with blossom and berry—
A woman with locks like the ripened corn,
  To a Southern cemetery.

The mounds swelled round like a summer sea
  Carressed by an in-shore wind;
Beyond, the stretch of an open lea,
  The shadowy forest behind.

Down by a grave with a bitter-sweet vine,
  Twining and trailing it over,
In the soft, rich glow of the morning's wine,
  She knelt in the nodding clover.

Knelt and bowed till the sad, white face
  Cozened the dew-starred grasses,
Still as a nun in some holy place
  When the Virgin spirit passes.

Screened by a vine at the self-same grave
  Was another figure kneeling,
With hair as white as the ocean's wave
  Before the hurricane reeling.

Their prayers are done and they rise as one—
  Each starts at sight of the other;
Said the younger: "This grave is the grave of
    my son."
  The elder: "Nay, I am his mother;

"I came o'er his ashes to weep and pray."
  The younger: "I tell you true,
My boy sleeps here, and he wore the gray."
  "Not so, but mine of the blue."

"There is some mistake," cried the gray-haired
    dame;
  Said she of the yellow braid:
"You'll find on the marble my dear boy's name,
  You surely have been betrayed."

They sought for the spot by the vines o'er-grown,
  And, crowding the leaves away,
Lo! two names carved in the mossy stone—
  The name of the blue and the gray.

One look they gave, then suddenly turned
  To clasp in a warm embrace—
The rising sun in its splendor burned,
  And glorified all the place.

The snow-white locks of the Northern land
  And the warm, rich Southern wave
In peace are mingled as hand in hand
  They kneel by the dual grave.

THE WATCHER BY THE SEA

Long years of watching have dimmed her eyes,
  That once were bright as stars i' the sea,
And over her temples, like snow-drift, lie
The locks that once were rich as the dye
  Of the purple grape on the tree.

She dwells in a cottage high o'ercrowned
  By cliffs that shadow the breakers white,
And Yule-tide, ever it comes around,
Still finds her waiting with holly bound,
Repeating with voice of tremulous sound,
" 'Tis Christmas Eve and the time is past,
The waiting and weeping are over at last,
  My rovers come home tonight.

"The bells will ring i' the hour, they said—
  Blow softly what winds may blow—
I have decked with holly my Robbie's bed,
That cosily stands in the room o'erhead,
  With its linen as white as snow—
As white as the snow on the window-sill—
As white as the snow that is lying still,
  On the still, white graves below.

"Graves! Only the feeble and old for graves!
 We are strong, we have naught to fear!
Comes the grand, good ship o'er the dancing waves
That brings to my bosom my rover braves,
 My mate and my boy so dear.

"My mate and my red-cheeked Robbie tonight
 Again in my arms shall meet,
And their thick curls gleam like gold i' the light
Of the fire that never will burn so bright
 As when they sit at my feet.

"He is ten years old when the clock strikes three—
 Our Robbie—he's growing old!
Last April it was that my mate and he—
Who says they will never come back to me?
 Ah, God, but the world is cold.

"I've waited so long—they will soon be here—
 Was that a step at the gate?
Or only the wind in the lilac near—
The wind that startles my soul with fear,
 The wind I worship—and hate?

"I dreamed—when was it?—a dream so dread—
 I saw myself sitting here,
Awaiting my loves, and there came instead
Some sailors bringing them in to me dead,
 Both dead on a single bier.

"With the drip, drip, drip of the salt sea brine,
    Drip, drip from their locks of gold;
In their cold blue eyes there was never a sign—
My dead mate clasping his boy and mine,
    As dead as himself and cold.

"A dream, but it chilled the founts of my soul,
    O, warm with their kisses I'll grow;
The bells are ringing—no, no, they toll!
Or is it the ocean's monotonous roll?—
    There is naught but a mound in the snow."

Long years of watching have dimmed her eyes,
    That once were bright as stars i' the sea,
And over her temples, like snow-drift, lie
The locks that once were rich as the dye
    Of the purple grape in the tree.

DISCOVERY

The jewel, Wisdom, in the mine of Thought
Lies bedded deep where toilers sore have wrought,
Or, be their search in old veins or in new,
The miners many, the discov'rers few.

AMBITION

Though many covetous be crowned,
  Their honors few with temperance wear;
The tree that tops the forest round
  Must brave the winds from every where.

HAPPY THE MAN

Happy the man who in some rural glade
  Contented dwells, nor of its confines tires;
The rich, sweet soil upturning with his spade
Where the dark earth, with little toil, is made
  To yield sufficient for his few desires.

The rush and turmoil of the greedy town,
  Its sin and pride and shame, to him unknown;
Nor beggar's whine, nor surly Mammon's frown;
Nor crack-voiced venders crying up and down,
  Nor drunkard's oath, nor ruined Virtue's moan.

Instead, the morning pulsing full with life,
  O'erflooded with the varied song of birds;
The pure, fresh air with scent of flowers rife—
Nor discord here, nor sound of sordid strife;
  But eloquence without disturbing words.

With swelling breast he roams the dewy meads,
  The meanest flow'r his joy and tender care;
The murm'ring winds that stir the tangled reeds,
Fit orchestra adapted to the needs
  Of Nature's drama acted for him there.

Of castle massive often he has read,
  Of mosque, of temple and cathedral grand—
Yet turns for beauty to the fields instead,
Finds some new pleasure wheresoe'er he tread,
  In meadow, wood or on the yielding sand.

The cliff abrupt; the river's silver flow;
　The eagle's flight; the tempest-ridden wind;
The gleaming salmon swinging to and fro
In quiet pool, the timid, graceful roe—
　All dear companions of his student mind.

For him the peace of close converse with God.
　To him the door of Nature opens wide;
The woods, the hills, the daisy-spangled sod,
He loves them all.　Where others blindly trod
　He moves serene—his being satisfied.

Amid such scenes his gentle life is passed,
　The ward of Wisdom, learning what is best;
His creed to love, his church the vaulted vast,
In contemplation richest at the last—
　He falls asleep upon a kindly breast.

REFLECTION

Where playful lamps serenely skip
O'er emerald green and blossomed slip,
A sage, with measured pace, came by
And marking all with dreamful eye,
Exclaimed, with tender, thoughtful smile:
"Poor creatures! but a little while
The grass will spring, the storm will rage,
Above the grave of lamb and sage.
The wise, the great, the reasonless,
The spangled sod alike shall press;
Your little hour of life you spend
In sportful pleasure; we extend
Our thought from this to other spheres
To win—a recompense of tears.
You hope not, doubt not, fear not; I
Do all by turns and yet must die
At last as ignorant as thou.
The studious mind but lines the brow
And stirs to bitter, fierce unrest
The flame-tongued forces in the breast.
All into one great Dark must grope
With but the flickering lamp of Hope
To guide them—as the fire-fly's light
Is to the thunder-clouded night,
E'en so it shows, now there, now here,
Now far removed, now blazing near,

An ignis fatuus while we stay,
What proof 'twill better lead the way
When, shorn of every subtle sense,
We plunge into the guessed Immense?"
The sage passed on to cry, "Alas!"
The lambkins nipped the tender grass.

INDUSTRY

The toughest wood with brightest blaze will greet:
The hardest nut contains the sweetest meat;
So wisdom, gained by light of midnight oil,
Gives richest recompense for patient toil.

BETWEEN THE WORLDS

I stand alone in the wind and rain
   As many another has stood,
O'er-brave with the light of a better life,
   And the sense of a higher good,
Yet feeling because of my sins as though
   The fire had gone out of my blood.
O Soul, thou art sobbing a sorrowful song,
   Like a brook in an Autumn wood!
When Faith would soar where the angels sing,
Doubt frowns, and she droops on a nerveless
    wing.

ON THE BORDER

We grew to manhood, Jim and I,
  Just where the border line
Cut through the homes of low and high
  As lightning cleaves the pine;
And from the passion-storm that swept
  The land from sea to sea
Two crafty tiger-spirits crept
  And parted him and me.

The South he loved was not so much,
  A languorous, dreamy girl,
And I, ah! well, I bear this crutch
  Because of one bright curl
That danced above a pair of eyes
  As mild as skies in May—
I donned the blue for Ann Elize,
  For Jess he took the gray.

A year went by, while cannons ploughed
  The fields our care had tilled;
Where seas of golden wheat had bowed
  A Nation's blood was spilled.
The sentry marched where love had stayed,
  And trampled meadows turned
Their brooks red-streaked into the glade
  Where hostile camp-fires burned.

The sweep of war had brought our lines
  Quite to the dear old spot,
And somehow in the whispering pines
  A song but half forgot—
A something half remembered drew
  Me out alone to roam
Along the path so well I knew
  Toward my boyhood's home.

Not mine alone to disregard
  The drums retiring taps—
Behold! Jim distant scarce a yard-   ·
  When we, two roguish chaps,
As ever caught the whistling rule
  Upon the shielding book,
Together held one bench at school,
  He wore the self-same look.

Two miles away, by marching spent,
  Slept eighty thousand men,
The brook, a silver ribbon went
  Full softly down the glen,
And stealing bright through leaf and bough
  The moon lit up the space
Where we, once friends, sworn foemen now,
  Stood silent, face to face.

My sword leaped naked to the night—
  Untouched his idly swung
Upon his thigh, but free and light
  His mellow laughter rung,

The while he cried, "Put up your steel,
  We'll fight what time we must,
Where cannons boom and squadrons wheel,
  And madmen bite the dust.

"But now, as comrade huntsmen come
  O'erwearied from the chase
Beyond the call of fife and drum,
  In this familiar place—
We'll sit us down and quiet chat
  Of simple, homelike joys,
Forgetful of the war and that
  We're anything but boys!"

I threw my sword upon the ground
  And grasped his proffered hand;
His voice just then the cheeriest sound
  In all the troubled land;
Then, stretched along the grassy slope,
  We watched the moon drift on,
And talked of home and love and hope
  Until the night was gone.

Next day the opposing forces met
  Midst smoke and roar and din,
And all the ground with blood was wet
  For Hate to struggle in,
While men, mere pawns to leaders wise,
  Of death made awful mirth,
And lids fell down o'er flashing eyes
  To lift no more on earth.

In charging through the dear old farm
    We met, friend Jim and I—
My saber shore him of an arm,
    His bayonet pierced my thigh.
Then all night long beneath the stars,
    We lay and moaned with pain—
If great men knew the cost of wars
    Would there be war again?

I have no heart to sing of strife;
    Each deed of valor done
Costs some brave fellow limb or life
    Or e'er the prize be won.
It likes me more in peace to dwell
    Among my fowl and kine,
Where Love, a sleepless sentinel,
    Keeps ward for me and mine.

And yet, while Ann Elize and Bill
    And Bess and little Sue
Are over yonder on the hill
    To drop a rose or two,
'Tis good to know that Jim and Jess,
    Down there in Tennessee,
Are tossing bloom of tenderness
    On those who fought with me.

TWILIGHT IN A CHURCH-YARD

Kneeling here beside thee, darling, while the twilight
softly steals
Like a nun, gray-veiled and quiet, from the cloister-
wood, and wheels
Through the heavens grand Orion—kneeling here at
eve alone,
Where the rose-bush clings and trembles round your
crumbling burial-stone;
Though my ears be dulled with hearing through long
years the din of life,
I can hear your voice as plainly as when first you mur-
mured "Wife,"—
Hear your voice as full and tender as the ringdove's
plaintive call
O'er the new-reaped clover meadow in the days of early
Fall.

O that life, so full of richness, bright as June beneath
the sky
Of the semi-tropics; heart-beats short the days flew
by;—
How the robin's pulsing treble seemed to voice the
love that swept
Through my being; closer, closer in your shielding
arms I crept;

Wishing nothing, fearing nothing, living only in the
  beam
Of your dear eyes bent above me.   Let the nighthawk
  swoop and scream;
What have I to fear!   The blackness of the darkness?
  Here I bide,
It is his dear voice that calls me, and I know he never
  died.

A CHRISTMAS CAROL

Ring out, ring out, ye choral bells,
  A paean to the morn;
Your speech in cadet measure tells
  Of blessings' newly born;
But be your tones as pure and clear
  As cloistered maiden's prayer,
For all of earth is listening here,
  And all of Heaven there.

Dear Christmas! enemy to fear
  And foe to sable sin,
Thou art the day of all the year
  For Joy to triumph in.
The hills are bathed in floods of gold,
  The frowning clouds are furled;
And cheerful sunlight, fold on fold,
  Enwraps a loving world.

The skies that bend to meet the sea
  Are softer on this day;
The winds that stir the holly tree
  Are gentler in their play;
The crystal flakes that kiss the earth
  Seem purer, whiter far,
The morning of our Savior's birth,
  Than other snow-flakes are.

Then ring, ye tongues of silver, ring
   Till tremble earth and sky!
Ye brazen throats, awake and sing
   A world-wide symphony!
'Neath every roof is white-robed Peace,
   And golden-haired and gray
Alike from care have full release—
   'Tis merry Christmas Day.

THROUGH A GLASS DARKLY

There's many a nobleman dwells in a cot,
  The palace holds many a clown,
And princes have beds of the tamarind bark,
  While beggars have couches of down.
Brave kings are in cotton, serfs glory in silk,
  While slaves like an emperor show;
For the worth of a title is stamped on the heart,
  But the world doesn't look at it so.

Here misers are prodigally flinging their gold
  To spendthrifts, who hoard in their wake;
There mumbles a rake in the gown of a priest
  To a priest in the garb of a rake;
Sweet saints there are living in hovels of sin,
  ,And sinners in Sanctified Row;
The heart in the breast is the only true test—
  But the world doesn't look at it so.

There are generals lying in graves unmarked,
  And privates with monuments grand;
The ignorant stalk in the chambers of state,
  While Virtue digs bread from the land.
A shadow divergent each object of earth
  O'ercast from one sun in the sky;
And fancies are many as beings have birth,
  But the one God ruleth on high.

So I laugh at the title; that's only a sham;
  And at caste—but a silver-washed plate
Stuck up on the door of a tenement grand
  Belonging to Nature's estate.
Its inmates are constantly changing and pass
  Each year out of sight, like the snow,
Whose going makes room for the beautiful bloom—
  And the Savior will look at it so.

WOMAN

Shut every door that leads to prosperous life;
He still hath hope who hath a helpful wife.
I liken woman to that fragile flow'r
That bends its head before the gentlest show'r,
But when the forest by the storm is lain
Looks brightly up to beautify the plain.

INNOCENCE

Scatter bright flowers on the grave of a child;
He with children was loving and mild,
Nothing they know of our sinful despair;
Scatter sweet roses and violets there.

THE AMERICAN FARMER

Shrill crows the cock. The misty light creeps in
　At windows looking on the eastern sky.
The cattle low and waking fowls begin
　To raise their voices in discordant cry,
When Farmer John, with many a lusty yawn,
Deserts his bed and stalks into the dawn.

With lib'ral hand he takes from stack and store,
　And, smiling, feeds his trooping flocks and herds,
Each known by name.　The weak he lingers o'er
　With soothing touch and kindly, cheering words.
From him they learn obedience and trust,
They teach him that the gentle are the just.

Compared to his what pleasures may they know
　Who in dull round of cent-per-cent engage?
About his feet the billowy grasses blow,
　E'en while the thunders o'er the hill-tops rage.
Here thick-leaved maples grateful shade extend,
There cowslip blossoms o'er the brooklet bend.

The sloping uplands clothed in emerald sheen,
　The solemn woods, the fields of velvet corn,
The clover meadows stretching gay between,
　The lark in carol to the dewy morn—
These, these are yours with all their clustering charms,
Steel-sinewed tillers of Our Country's farms. ,

And here among these rich, sequestered scenes,
  An independent, peaceful path you tread;
No tainting substance e'er your sky terrenes,
  No marshaled chimneys turn your airs to lead
Above you bends a blue, unsullied dome;
The sun unveiled looks smiling on your home.

MEMORIAL MORNING

"Virginia, open the casement there,
    I hear the sound of a martial band
In the street below. Let me catch the air.
    The doctor? How; shall *I* not command?

"There, child, forgive me; old age is quick
    To anger, in patience a very snail;
But I'll to the window; life's shriveled wick
    Shall blaze once more ere it utterly fail.

"Ah! so; the curtain a trifle down.
    Ho! Halt you there where the sunlight plays
So merrily over your locks of brown—
    They had just such curls in the dear old days.

"My sweet twin darlings. It cannot be—
    What's that they are playing? 'The Tender and
        True?'
You are like your father as like can be,
    And they both come back to me, both in you.

"They are not forgotten! The Nation halts
    In its greedful rush for an hour or so
To shrive itself of its baser faults,
    Lest it altogether forgetful grow.

"Nay, nay, I am querulous; thoughts like these
  Dishonor Love's festal, and surely I
Should honor a custom that strips the trees '
  For love of the dead who are not to die.

"For yonder, where Donnelson frowns above
  The Cumberland waters, my darlings rest
In each other's arms—in the clasp of love,
  Where they fell, my heroes, fell breast to breast.

"God sits in judgment! To honor bound
  Were both my boys, though they walked apart,
But they sleep today 'neath a single mound,
  Sleep shoulder to shoulder and heart to heart.

"As in one low cradle they used to sleep,
  My blush-rose babies. What, tears, my child?
For the Nation's dead let the Nation weep,
  And kneeling above them be reconciled!

"If palm leaves whispered their lullaby,
  Or North winds shouted their cradle song,
What matter? Their duty to do and die;
  Their deeds, not motives, to us belong.

"What to me, if the flags that my darlings bore
  Were barred and spangled or azure thread,
If blue or gray were the coats they wore?
  They were all my world and—my world is dead.

"Where mounds are many go scatter your flowers,
  Ye prosperous people; where mounds are few,
Where the lone loon calls to the lonely hours,
  Where the sensitive aspen-tree scatters the dew.

"On plain or mountain, by river or wood,
  Wherever a soldier is sleeping today,
Let fall the blossoms in fragrant flood—
  They are sons of one mother, the Blue and the Gray."

THANKSGIVING HYMN

Spirit of love! Creator! Ruler! Friend!
From whom we come and unto whom we tend!
All humbly now, Thy presence drawing near,
We sing Thanksgiving for the fruitful year.
Thy gracious care in every good is seen!
Beneath Thine eyes the planets move serene,
Spring, Summer, Autumn, following in their round,
With rich abundance rural toil is crowned;
The seeds that fell along the hillside bare,
A thousand-fold returned, demand our care;
With soothing cud the meadows yet supply
The browsing herd; the clover's rafter high
Above the stalls—beneath contented feed
Sleek, fattening steer and glossy-coated steed.
Devout of heart, we here our thanks renew
To Thee who gave the sun, the rain and dew.

Thanks, too, for these! the anvil's hearty ring;
The merry lathes that labor as they sing;
The wheezing plane, the saw, the plumb, the rule,
And every useful, honor-bearing tool
That may on man one comfort more bestow—
I'll sing them still and ay my verse shall flow.

Now double blessings to the generous man
Who measures Nature by the liberal plan!
Upright and honest; of forgiving mind,

E'er thoughtful of his less successful kind;
Prompt in his action; just in his decrees,
Pleased most to see a fellow-being pleased;
Ne'er over proud because his ventures float;
Who judges not his fellow by the coat,
But cries: "Let's prove the heart that throbs beneath!
Damascus blade has oft a ragged sheath,
While swords of lead in gorgeous scabbard shine;
The dearest metal's from the deepest mine.
By honeyed accents greatest kingdoms fall;
The dress is nothing, but the *man* is all!
Go! Give thy thanks! Not as the Pharisee,
But in your closet on an humble knee."

What comfort should we bring to grieving hearts
Did we but act as we do know our parts;
How much regret ourselves, ourselves would spare
If what we win we might with temperance wear!
Proud, halting, weak! O God, of all above!
Still be Thy justice tempered by Thy love.

WELL DONE

For fifty years as man and wife
  They traveled on together;
Between them not a word of strife
  In fair or cloudy weather.

Full fifty years thro' sun and storm,
  With cares and griefs a-plenty,
But fourscore found their love as warm
  And tender as at twenty.

They learned each other's failings, yet,
  Ne'er halting to compare them,
Strove still with patience to forget
  Or cheerfully to bear them.

The loving are the truly wise
  And Wisdom counsels grieving;
When tears of sorrow dimmed their eyes
  They dried them with believing.

Strong in that self-respecting pride
  Which only is deserving—
From Duty never turned aside,
  They kept her path unswerving.

As dual tendrils intertwined
  Will perish being parted,
E'en so, his day of life declined,
  She followed, broken-hearted.

One marble marks their resting place,
  And all their story telling,
"Well done," the simple words that grace
  The stone above their dwelling.

A vine sprung from the hallowed ground—
  O may it ne'er be blighted!—
In death unites them mound to mound,
  As love in life united.

Where swallows through the ether glide,
  Where nods the fragrant clover—
  The waving, scented clover—
They sleep in quiet side by side
  Their toils and trials over.

LOVE IS NEVER OLD

Have your footsteps lost the lightness
   That in other days they knew?
Have your eyes forgot their brightness,
   And your locks their raven hue?
Ah! the years are many, darling,
   Since we first the story told;
But 'tis sweet today as ever—
   Love is never old.

From your cheeks the baby fingers
   Plucked the roses one by one,
But the precious fragrance lingers
   When the flower itself is gone;
And those hands, grown strong and sturdy,
   Keep us from the storm and cold,
Lead us by the peaceful waters—
   Love is never old.

CRITICISM

"There's something hidden in the book,"
  I said; "some meaning, subtle, strange.
I'll search it out though I should look
Behind each word, scan every nook
    Within the author's range."

    Her fingers smoothing back my hair
  Were still for just a second, then
A voice as musical as air
  Replied: "Alas! like other men,
You crush the dearest buds that grow
  Along the 'broidered walks of life,
In search of flowers that never blow;
In search of that which never grew
Despoil a thousand drops of dew,
And climb the tree for fruit less sweet
Than that which tumbles at your feet.
Because a rosebud pleases one,
Must he uproot it in the sun
To find wherein its fragrance lies,
,Or note the meaning of its dyes?
Good writers, read by kindred minds,
Have nothing hidden in their lines;"
    Thus answered me my wife.

THE APPROACH OF WINTER

The laggard morning tints a ragged East,
  The sun a red and rayless disk appears;
While baffled vapors, fresh from pois'nous feast,
  The uplands moisten with revengeful tears.

A watchful crow swings cawing from the wood,
  A lonely mallard flutters from the brake,
And Nature, clad in somber cloak and hood,
  Stirs languidly as she were loth to wake.

The leaves that lately shone so fresh and bright,
  Now dry and withered, to the ground are cast;
Where ever round and round in restless flight
  They're driven by the chill November blast.

The sumac in the naked hedgerow bleeds,
  Impatiently the blue jay calls his mate;
A crane stalks ghostly through the swaying reeds,
  And Autumn mourns her kingdom desolate.

RETRIBUTION

At last you are home from the carnival? I—
By my faith, 'tis a regal head—
Have been pondering here, as the hours went by,
On the fleshless hand and the rayless eye—
    List, madam, our child is dead.

Is dead, I tell you—asleep, asleep.
    Keep silence and wake her not!
I watched her going, but did not weep,
And devils came out of the shade to peep
    At the one bright crimson spot—

You would see our darling? 'Twill be as well.
    So, lay the jewels aside,
And all these shimmering robes that tell
Of the stately measure and cadent swell,
    Of the sinuous sweep and glide

Of the amorous waltz. Am I harsh? And thou,
Oh, gentle and loving mind!
With thy jeweled throat and thy painted brow—
And have you reason to chide me now
    With cruelty? I unkind!

                *   *   *   *   *   *   *   *

It likes me better, this simple dress;
    What a small, small throat, my love!
Do you shrink from my touches of tenderness?

Time was you were hungry for each caress,
  And cooed in return like a dove.

We will go together, and you may weep—
  Your breath—my fingers are steel!
O'er that silent couch with its snow-white heap
Of marble beauty in breathless sleep.
  What, Love! you falter and reel!

So well I loved her, *our* child, my dear—
  What say you? Believe, you true?
And she was so pretty I had a fear
The world might claim her and leave me here
  Alone when she older grew.

And I rocked her asleep in my shielding arms
  (Did you dance with the count tonight?)
I rocked her, and whispered: The world's alarms
Shall never come near you, nor shall your charms
  Grow pale in a lover's sight.

And I said I would keep her, the bloom on her
    cheeks—
  There, still as the child you've grown,
And white as the snow on the mountain peaks,
Soft by our little one—ha! who speaks?
  I have had my way with my own.

WHEN THE GRIP IS IN THE LOFT

O the sweet and blissful feelings that possess the drum-
    mer's breast
When the year's last trip is over and he nears the
    promised rest!
O the happy fancies rushing—as the children rush from
    school
When, the tiresome lesson finished, they are freed from
    book and rule!
Happy fancies crowding, tripping o'er the threshold
    of his heart
To the playground just before him—how his pulses
    thrill and start
E'en to think the cares of roaming, for the time at least,
    are doffed
And the battered grip will linger for a season in the
    loft.

To be freed from hours of waiting for the long belated
    train
And the call-boy's piping treble e'er he's scarce an hour
    lain
Tired head upon the pillow slipping always to the
    floor,
Quite as if its fragile system couldn't stand a healthful
    snore—
And the dreamy, dreary calling of the trainman's nasal
    tones,

With his "All a-b-o-a-r-d-fer-D-a-v-e-n-p-o-r-t,
O-m-a-h-a an' Fre-m-o-n-e-s!"
Ah, the drummer's voice is gentle and the drummer's
heart is soft
As he tosts the battered gripsack for a season to the
loft.

Onward glides the stream of pleasure all unbroken in
its flow—
There are days to romp with Nellie and the chubby
toddler Joe;
There are long and quiet evenings in the parlor neat
and trim
Which his dear, observant Mary's furnished with an
eye to him;
Time to tell again the story that is ever new and sweet
With a pleasant sense of knowing there is one secure
retreat
Where the lusty-lunged train-caller, with his grandly
swelling chest
Dare not shout "Yer now fer Davenport, O-m-a-h-a
an' der West"—
If the drummer isn't married he is certainly betrothed
And the parlor 's quite as pleasant when the grip is
in the loft.

There will come a day my comrades—it is well to note
it here
While we're taking stock of conduct with the closing
of the year—
When the old familiar places will no more our faces
see

And there'll be no sweet vacations kept by either you
  or me.

There will come an end of wand'ring up and down this
  world of sin

When the Author of all drummers will have called our
  samples in—

When the lusty-lunged train-caller with his grandly
  swelling chest

Crying "All a-b-o-a-r-d fer Davenport, O-m-a-h-a, an'
  the West!"

Won't have power to wake the sleeper he before has
  wakened oft,

And the battered grip will nevermore be taken from the
  loft.

EASTER PROMISES

"There is no death?" the flowers say
"In faith we hide our souls away,
While tempests desolate the earth.
And patient wait the promised birth."

The south wind chants, "There is no death,
I come and winter is a breath:
Against his falling walls I set
The snowdrop and the violet."

Glad prophets of the life to be,
A kindred spark abides in me,
That, like the wind, no tether knows,
And yet is comrade to the rose.

Thus mother earth, thy gracious breast
Gives all thy tired children rest,
Where, sheltered from the storms they bide
The coming of the Easter tide.

THE SPIRIT OF SILENCE

From a mansion window in careless way
Were tossed the roses of yesterday.

But a breath of their fragrance drifted in
Where a sick man lay—worn, pale, and thin.

And the Spirit that builded, so long ago,
The wise king's temple awoke, and lo!

With never a sound would have stirred the thread
That grows in the wake of a spider's tread,

Stone, brick, and mortar were swept aside,
And the sick man strolled by a meadow wide,

O'er a low-hung ridge where the blue-joint tips
Reach up till they beat at the passer's hips.

A bluebird hopped on the topmost rail
Of a zigzag fence, and a distant quail

Called silvery clear: "More wet, more green!"
Though never a cloud in the sky was seen.

A drunken bobolink swayed and reeled
O'er the yellow sea of a barley-field;

Rang sweet the song of a joy-mad thrush;
And a wild rose turned with a modest blush,

From the wooing bold of the cat-bird's drawl;
The air was stilled with the cricket's call;

And the man passed into the greenwood shade
While the Spirit of Silence the town re-made.

The tide of commerce roared over the bloom,
And they covered the face in the darkened room

Where the watchers wept, for the world is blind,
But the Spirit of Silence is wise and kind.

THE GOSPEL OF REST.

I watched them jostling in eager strife—
(Locks of auburn and locks of gray)ʾ
Faces grown old with the cares of a life,
Faces grown old with a day.

And I paused to question, What better, O slave,
　Fast chained to the loom, when the web is spun
And the cloth of your weaving scarce covers a grave—
　What better when all is done?

Is it better to delve in the dust of trade,
　Close hugging its gold with a miser's greed?
Or roam a barbarian free in the shade,
　Unfettered by law or creed?

To plunge in the sea where the breakers roar,
　Or sit on the sand where the wave sings low?
To trouble the river with noisy oar—
　Or drift with its quiet flow?

Is it better to labor the long day through—
　(The hope, elusive, is ne'er fulfilled)
Or loiter in shadow as dumb kine do,
　Let the field be fallow or tilled?

The ark of wisdom may sometime keep
  From the flood of sorrow, the man of care,
But Noahs will lie in the sun asleep,
  And only the few be fair.

What better to burden the sportive brain
  With subtle reasoning—dim the eyes
With constant seeking? Lo! yonder plain
  Breathes joy to the smiling skies.

Go roam where the nightingale sings to his mate!
  Where the moon spills silver in dusky pool!
The heart of the wanderer laughs at fate
' If his feet with the dews be cool.

The beautiful butterfly, leaving its cell,
  Leaps up to the sun from the sun-baked wall;
Get wings! If the worm may despise the shell,
  What need for the man to crawl?

Is living a lesson so hard to learn
  That we still are writing the task in tears?
Let the gray dove mourn and the lone owl yearn,
  What are these to the song of the spheres?

I watched them jostling in eager strife—
  (Locks of auburn and locks of gray)
Faces grown old with the cares of a life,
  Faces grown old with a day,

And I paused to question, What better, O slave,
   Fast chained to the loom, when the web is spun
And the cloth of your weaving scarce covers a grave—
   What better when all is done?

THE SINGER WHOM NOBODY KNOWS

There's a dear little singer come out of the West,
   A singer whom nobody knows;
The weary have only to listen and rest:—
   If biting old Boreas blows
She pictures the gladness that Summer-time brings—
   The violets under the snows,
Till the air is alive with the rustle of wings—
   The singer whom nobody knows.

She lightens the burden of toiler opprest,
   The singer whom nobody knows;
She coaxes despair from the wanderer's breast.
   Her verse so melodious flows
It sweetens the speech of the slanderous tongue,
   It chastens the prodigal's woes,
And soothes the poor bosom by perfidy wrung—
   The singer whom nobody knows.

I would I might find her, this lyrical bee,
   This singer whom nobody knows;
'Though plain as a sparrow, as charming to me
   As the delicate breath of a rose.
Oh, precious her harvest, if so it be true
   That the Spirit shall reap as it sows,
For she's bringing in lilies and casting out rue—
   The singer whom nobody knows.

THE BETTER BIRTH

Two came to the sexton at early morn,
  A peasant and servant of the king.
The servant: "Ring, sexton, a glad acclaim:
  A son is born to his Majesty, ring!"
The peasant: "O sexton I pray you toll,
  My boy is dead." And the graybeard smiled,
While he rang a chime for the care-freed soul,
  And tolled for the king-born child.

THE SOUL OF LIFE IS LOVE.

The world is as a sterile cliff;
  But love is like the dew
That falls upon it, and the moss,
  Like life, springs from the two.
    It creepeth o'er the barren stone
    Till all the place be verdant grown.

The world is as a blasted oak,
  But love is like the vine
That trails it o'er; its sunlit leaves,
  Like life, the two entwine.
    The trunk is green that erst was bare,
    And blossoms kiss it everywhere.

The world is as a clouded sea,
  But love is like the sun
That steals along the murky waves
  And brightens every one.
    O'er gloom is golden glory flung
    While sunbeams sport the waves among.

SWEET ROCK-A-BY

Rock-a-by baby, my pink and white cherub,
Droop little lids o'er the questioning eyes,
Angels will guard theē and sweeten thy slumber,
Rock-a-by, lullaby, pink and white prize.
Into the land of the soft flowing water,
Fairies and flowers and slow waving bough,
Steal away baby, my pink and white rosy,
Mamma is rocking thee, sleep baby, now.

Mamma is rocking thee, lovingly rocking thee,
Rock-a-by baby, my sweet, rock-a-by.

Where will you wander, my pink and white beauty?
Is it to heaven in dreams you will stray?
'Twas only yesterday, pink and white rosy,
Only but yesterday you came away;
Now could I follow where soul-wings are wafting—
Follow thy dreaming, O what should I see?
Sleep, darling, sleep, and thy slumber over,
Bring back thy visions, my baby, to me.

Mamma is rocking thee, lovingly rocking thee,
Rock-a-by baby, my sweet, rock-a-by.

LONG YEARS AGO

Long years ago, on arid ground,
Beside a rocky ledge, I found
    A tiny flower in bloom;
The desert, bleak and bare and gray,
All verdureless about us lay,
    Curled as the hand of doom
Had touched and shriveled it; alone
The flower bloomed above the stone—
    A star above a tomb.

Tonight, inquisitive of mood,
I wandered where the demon brood
    Of want and hunger wait;
Where worth is sacrificed to might,
And wanton creatures curse the Light
    In hovels desolate;
Where ribald song and mocking jest,
And shifting gaze and sunken chest
    Proclaim the Fiend's estate.

And there in that discordant din,
The heavy air red-ribbed with sin,
    I found a toddling child
With face as pure and sweet and fair

As e'er was fanned by Heaven's air,
　As angel's undefiled.
'Lo! Thou art everywhere," I cried;
"And love will bloom where love hath died,
　To cheer the bleakest wild."

COLUMBUS

Hail! hail! hail! Mighty navigator!
Hail! hail! hail! Prophet of the free!
Creed and kingdom crumbling fall,
Liberty enlightens all
    Now because of thee—
    Columbus! Columbus!
    All because of thee.

Hail! hail! hail! Messenger of wisdom!
Hail! hail! hail! Worthy child of Fame!
Blare of trumpet, roll of drum—
Ho, the Nations crowding come
    Chorusing thy name,
    Columbus! Columbus!
    Chorusing thy name.

THE DEAD CROESUS

He knew the scientific name
　Of every hot-house flow'r
And in their glass-walled company
　He lingered many an hour.
But where the lowly violet
　Bloomed bravely in the snow
He never came; its humble ways
　He did not care to know.

And now he's dead; of all his gold
　(So well he loved it, too,)
Not one poor penny's worth enclasp
　The fingers cold and blue.
The violet, sweet heaven's charge,
　Fills all the world beyond—
But not one hybrid blossoms there
　Of which he was so fond.

THE NEW PARSON

Yes, parson, you're studied in books, no doubt,
  But when the heart is a-longin' to pray,
  We don't consider what's best to say;
There's a feelin' behind just a-crowdin' it out.

Your preachin' has got us somehow unstrung;
  An' just when our feelin's beginnin' to wake,
  Some furrin lingo creeps in t' break
The spell; we feel in our mother tongue.

We ain't a-hungerin' for Latin an' Greek,
  What we want, parson, is reason an' truth,
  The good old kind that we larned in youth;
An' a simple language we all can speak.

Your intentions is good, but your high-flown terms
  An' logic—no doubt o' the very best—
  Don't seem to lull us to peaceful rest,
We listen and feel we are ignorant worms.

The trout swims deep when the fishhawk calls;
  The thrush is oftenest found in the thorn;
  The scarecrow's better'n a rose in the corn;
An' the rainbow shines where the water falls.

A star is brighter seen through the trees,
    An' God is nearer in storm than sun;
    It tenders the heart an' it softens the tone
To feel that He with His own agrees;

That back of all trouble a Glorious Power
    Still leaves an' blossoms the bleak, bare grove;
    The vine climbs higher'n the tree for His love;
The same as we mortals in tryin' hour.

An' so believin' you can't think strange
    If we plod along in our simple way
    The little time that we have to stay,
An' don't go huntin' about for change.

Now don't be angered at what I've said.
    Go right on, parson, an' pray an' preach
    In a natural way an' a natural speech,
An' let the dead languages rest with the dead.

WHO SHALL JUDGE

God made the Universe and hurled
It forth to being, world on world.
As hopefully the inventive boy
Sets spinning his new-fashioned toy—
But with this difference—Nature wrought
Perfection from a perfect thought,
And as 'tis true the spinning top
Must, from its imperfections, stop,
So true the world, of perfect plan,
Will on forever. Dreaming man
Sees only by imperfect light—
Clear all things to the Infinite.
Poor, blind humanity must feel
Its way through life; and woe and weal,
E'er winding pathways, near allied,
Running forever side by side,
What wonder man so often strays
From that to this throughout his days!
Today we deem ourselves sin-proof,
And from the wayward hold aloof—
Tomorrow flounder deep in woes
While he we spurned straight onward goes.
The heart is truest, noblest, best,
That makes a brother's grief its guest;
That gives to famished souls a feast
And judgeth of its neighbor least.

The humble toiler trills along
And lightens labor with a song—
The worshipers of Mammon sneer
Because, mayhap, the poet's ear
Hath caught the harmonies that roll
In rhythmic cadence round his soul,
Forgetful of the pen and brain
That gave the toiler his refrain.
And poet, gentle still of heart,
Sighs thoughtful, as he turns apart—
"I'd rather be a lark and sing
My song on free, empyreal wing,
O'er-happy if, in Sorrow's throng
One heart be lighter for the song,
Than tuneless lord of boastful birth
To banish Peace and throttle Mirth.
And if at eve my pulsing breast
To damp and chilly heath be prest,
And frowning skies my comfort blight,
I'll spring as gay at morning's light
And pour my rippling melody
Out o'er the field as full and free
As though a thousand fairies strove
To make my couch as warm as love."

Thus minds, as planets, circle 'round,
And Truth 'twixt opposites is found—
Thus every being bears a part
To stir the blood in Nature's heart.
And, when at last this wordly guise
Shall vanish in the light of eyes

True, perfect, clear as He shall give,
'Twill be our destiny to live
Where by heart is clearly read,
And, howsoe'er our paths we tread,
So shall we sup of woe or bliss
In that world, as we love in this.
And He, of all the life and soul,
Must view His product onward roll
Forever. For the worlds that be
Swim in an everlasting sea.

STRENGTH OF SIMPLICITY

"Blow!" cried a lordly oak. "I brave
    The winds from everywhere!"
A wood-flower in its shadow gave
    A shiver of despair.
The tempest woke. The forest kings
        Tost in the clouds their locks,
And through the skies, on wings of flame,
The thunder-gods contending came:—
        The tempest slept. The flower looked up,
        A rain drop shining in its cup—
        The oak lay on the rocks.

ALONE

The moon is waning in the sky
  (My steps are feeble grown and slow)
I see the lazy dragon-fly
On gaudy wing go sailing by—
  How chill the evening zephyrs grow.

I watch the brown leaves twirl and fall—
  Fall down and flee on Autumn's breath;
I hear the mournful ring-dove's call.
The plover's cry, and each and all
  Bear solemn prophecies of death.

Oh could my heart have drunk the draught
  Vouchsafed to some while shone the day,
Death's cup I then had willing quaffed,
Aye, drank the very dregs and laughed
  To see him cheated of his prey.

Could I have had assurance sweet
  From but one soul in all the throng,
That in the future, weary feet,
Heavy with labor, should grow fleet
  Because my muse had sung one song!

But no, not mine this joy. My days
  (Some buds there are which never ope)
Have borne me in such darkened ways
That, though I ever strain my gaze
  For light, I still in darkness grope.

O Thou to whom I bend the knee,
  The stars and birds alike Thy care;
Touch Thou mine eyes that I may see.
Alone 'tis ever night, with Thee
  'Tis glorious morning everywhere.

AB EXTRA

"There are no poor—thank God!" I cried and turned
  To see a burdened woman trembling fare,—
The strands of trouble silvering her hair—
Slow from the shop close hugging what she'd earned:
I saw the bundle that had been her task,
A thousand stitches pearled with anxious tears,
      And all her pay,
          Food for a day,
The putting forward just so far her fears,—
"Let us give thanks, He answereth all who ask!"

"Thanksgiving for Thy blessings manifold!"
  So rang the anthem and the righteous bow'd
  Within the church. Without, a blue-lipped crowd,
Half-clad, half-fed, stood shivering with cold.
  "Give us to do your drudgery," they plead,
"That we may eat." "There is a store of bread."
The parson cried, "Give thanks, and prayer and praise,
  His sheep have come into their own at last,
  Have fallen on the full, delightful days—"
"Give us to eat!" again the rabble cried,
  The parson, softly—"For the poor He died."

"Thanksgiving!" cry the favored, "God is good!"
The hovels tremble with the groans for food.

DAWN AND DUSK

Where all-year skies are blue and bright,
    And pour the moonbeams golden
O'er flow-ring fields in floods of light—
    Where rambling houses olden
Throw wide their doors on spacious halls
    And roomy chimneys brighten,
In autumn days, the pictured walls,
    Where songs harmonious lighten
The dusky toiler's burden; where
    The mocking bird makes cheery
With every vagrant warbler's air,
    'Twas there I met my dearie.

The zephyrs through the nodding pines
    Were musically stealing,
The blossoms drifted from the vines
    That up the oaks were reeling;
There, while the thrush sang overhead,
    Our tender vows we plighted—
And solemn words were softly said,
    That our young lives united.

Long years we've journeyed side by side,
    And all the hours are golden
As moonbeams that through portals wide,
All beautiful and silent glide
    Into the mansion olden.

O, COME WITH ME

O come with me to the wild-wood free
  Where the south wind fetterless blows;
Where the nymphs peep out with a saucy pout
  From the tips of the budding rose.
Where the zephyrs play on their scented way,
  And the boughs with their tones are rife,
Where voices I know will whisper us low
  From the soul of their secret life.

O come with me where the thrush goes mad
  With joy of the summer's glow,
And the squirrel calls from the orchard walls,
  And the time has never a no.

Where the brook leaps up to the leaf-formed cup,
  And the mandrake nods in the shade,
Where the blackberries peep from the coverts deep,
  And the wild bees' hoard is made.
From the mad town come where the partridge drum
  Goes echoing down the glen.
Let the crowd go by—it is moan and sigh
  And curse in the haunts of men.

Then come with me where the thrush goes mad
  With joy of the summer's glow,
Where the squirrel calls from the orchard walls,
  And the time has never a no.

THE SILENT LAND

God's language tells us we are One,
And somewhere, 'twixt the stars and sun,
The Vale of Peace in quiet lies,
Where human hearts grow truly wise;
Where gliding spirits feed the mind
With truth; where souls are not confined
To narrow paths, but roam at will
O'er mead and mountain, heath and hill;
In fair Tacita's waters lave,
And, living, rest as in the grave.
A land wherein the woeful word
That blinds the thought is never heard,
But soul with soul hath converse sweet,
In language soundless, full, complete.
Who enters there leaves speech behind,
But mind, illumined, reads the mind.
The gleaming walls that skirt it round
Have never heard the voice of sound;
Yet paeans swell and anthems roll
Harmonious—music of the soul.
To live will be to understand
When we have gained the Silent Land.

IN DIFFERENT MEASURE

"Laugh and the world laughs with you."—Ella Wheeler Wilcox

O, sing to the priestess of unrestrained pleasure,
  Laugh till the walls of the palace resound!
Dainty shoon beat out the rhythmical measure,
  Wine glasses tinkle and leap at the sound!
Crown her with roses, voluptuous red ones,
  Bring in the bacchanals, slaughter the calf—
Poverty's wailing its dying and dead ones?
  Teach it, dear poetess, teach it to laugh.

Long have we waited her muse to enroll us
  Angels of mercy the foremost and best:
Others for ages refused to extol us—
  Singing forever the poor and oppressed.
Homer to Burns! They did naught but abuse us,
  Flailing with wit our pretentions to chaff,
She is the first to redeem us and choose us
  The theme for a song—to delight in our laugh.

Laugh and the world will laugh with you! Be cheery;
  Thrust back that sob on your womanish heart!
Others have hovels as empty and dreary,
  Others have babes 'neath the Juggernaut cart—

There is no treachery, knavery, sorrow,
  Throw down the crutches and discard the staff,
Put by your hunger, 'twill keep till tomorrow,
  Be deaf to the wailing of others and laugh.

THE PESSIMIST

Before him sweeps the cavalcade of Space;
Behind him tramps the cavalry of Time;
And 'twixt the two, with hopeless, aging face,
He struggles through a *chapparral* of crime.

POOR OLD WORLD

Poor old world, thy sun's declining;
  'Twixt thy two extremes a door
Darkling shuts—within the dining,
  And without the starving poor.
Bankrupt all! We've banished pleasure,
  Passion rules the hearts of men—
In the palace hoarding treasure
  Cursing treasure in the den.

Fled the saintly triple Graces,
  Fled their gentle sister Peace;
Gold has flattened human faces
  By the weight of its increase.
Every lofty thought is smothered,
  Dead is Friendship's generous glow—
See the race by Freedom mothered
  Unto Mammon bowing low.

JUNE

Most welcome, thou of lavish hand!
A subtle fragrance fills the land;
The sea is silver, and the strand
      A wave of gold;
The fruit peeps forth on every hand,
      And flowers unfold.

The verdant hills are proud to wear
Thy blushing favors, and declare
Thy purpled richness. Everywhere
      Is glory spread,
And tree and shrub and earth and air
      To beauty wed.

THE FALLEN LEAF

From its brothers gay on the boughs at play—
  Like the tear of a hidden grief
O'er the cheek of care—through the lambent air
  Slow-drifted an idle leaf.
    .

To be caught at last by the brook that passed
  And sang to the boughs above,
Where it rose and fell with the dip and swell,
  Like a brooch at the throat of love.

Then out on the stream, with a saucy gleam,
  It was swept by the current down
Where the mists of grey from the rapids' play
  Are pied with the rocks of brown.

Oh! the leaves that fall at the frost-king's call,
  They are mourned as the dead may be,
But the one astray—how the home-hearts pray
  For that one on the Somewhere Sea.

LIBERTY BELL AT THE WORLD'S FAIR

Grand old bell, thy earlier mission but to voice on Sab-
    bath morning—
    As an angel's fingers pressed thee,
    As an angel's wings caressed thee,
    Softly chiming from the steeple,
    "Rest ye, rest ye, O my people!"
In mellifluous tones and tender with an undertone of
    warning,—
    Changed thy speech, as all men know,
    On that morning long ago,
    When thy stern majestic ring
    Bade defiance to a king.

In the streets are gathered thousands waiting for the
    message grand
That shall loose their bonds and make them freemen
    in a freeman's land,—
    That shall by a single motion
    Send defiance o'er the ocean,
    Signal ships are outward pointed,
      Signal ships that homeward run,
    That a prince by priest anointed
      Is but man when all is done.

Brave men breathless stand below thee, pale of cheek
    but stern of brow,
Praying for th' proclamation—moments are as hours
    now,

See! the hand uplifted wavers,
    Falls—the bellman straining there,
Sends the song on rhythmic quavers
    Out upon the dancing air,
"They have signed it, O my people!"
Cries the bell from out the steeple,
"Independence! Independence! Liberty is newly
    crowned!"
Chorus all the waiting thousands till the old bell's voice
    is drowned.

But that glorious proclamation,
    Swiftly everywhere it ran
And demanded of each nation
    Equal rights for every man.

How the spirit of Columbia into every heart has grown
    Best is told by yon White City—symbolizing all that's
    good.
East and West are come together—there is neither pole
    nor zone,
    There is neither slave nor monarch; but where late
    the willow stood,
Stands the wonder of the ages. Stroke the old bell's
    rusty side,
    Right has triumphed and before her cowers Tyranny
    and Pride.

UNREWARDED

To sing, that seemed his one delight,
  Betrayed of man, he sang for men,
O'erfilled with gladness if he might
  But win the sad to smile again;
Poor in those things the mean adore,
  Rich in those things the gods revere,
He scattered largess from his store—
  The world repaid him with a sneer.

Ah, bright the face of Hope appears
  To those by sad mischance distrest—
A sun that rainbows falling tears,
  A moon that swims in Trouble's breast.
But cruel fortune left him blind—
  She gave the cross, but kept the crown—
He wrote his name upon the wind
  And weighted it with thistledown.

THE COMING DAY

You do not see the tears fall,
     O scoffers
     With coffers
In which you lock your hearts;
You do not see the mists that lie
Before the ever-yearning eye
     When peace from life departs.

You do not see the blood flow
     O blind ones,
     Unkind ones,
     Who hoard the shining dust;
You do not know the grief they feel
Who through a night of anguish kneel
     Praying to keep their trust.

Yet they are all about you,
     The falling ones
     The calling ones,
     Here, there, they fainting lie;
O when at last your steps are stayed
And you are low beside them laid,
     Can you for mercy cry?

If e'er the burden-bearing
    Shall cease to pray.
    Beware the day,
    Sweet princes, boasting much!
The lion ravened of her young
Is gentler than the human stung
    Beyond Hope's healing touch.

CLOTHES WORSHIP

The world will crack the devil o'er the pate
If, dressed in rags, he peep above the gate—
But let the velvet hide his cloven hoof,
He finds a welcome under every roof.

THE GOOD IN EVERYTHING

I ain't jes' got my bearin's on these Socialistic facts,
An' I'm summat undecided 'bout the scheme o' Single
Tax,
But all year round I'm pulling strong with any man ur
creed
'At gits a crowd together fur a feller-bein's need.
I ain't sot on no theury, nur any special plan
To bring about redemption. T' me the average man
Is puz'lin' es a gol' mine—so many slants an' shifts—
Ain't like to strike it payin' till y've run a dozen drifts;
But one thing now I know es well es any man a-talkin',
The bad ain't all in kerriges, nur all the gu'd a-walkin'.

Take my ole mare—o' humble birth—she'd never
captur' Bonner,
But fleet Maud S., pert—speedy tew—with all her gew-
gaws on her,
'Ud never pull me half so safe. I take more comfort
with her
A joggin' through the pastur' lan's an' long the shaded
river,
Than he can git a-flyin' o'er a road o' powdered mortar
An' feelin' 'at his nag don't pass es many es she'd
orter—
But both on 'em ha' got their pints thar ain't no sulks
nur balkin'—
The bad ain't all in kerriges, nur all the gu'd a-walkin'.

That's few on us 'll edge t' square, fur Natur' runs t'
    bevels,
But if there is a dearth o' saints thar ain't so many
    devils.
The truth is, minor strains o' gu'd run through the
    most o' cre'tur's—
We ain't all han'sum, but we've all got some redeemin'
    fe'tur's;
An' when y' come across a man 'et seems supremely
    bad,
Jes' fin' the stone 'et's shuttin' out the sunshine frum
    the lad,
An' if you len' a kin'ly han' t' roll that stone away,
You'll see a shoot come peepin' up t' greet th' cheerin'
    day,
An' spreadin' out its tiny han's, an' by an' by 't'll
    bloom,
An' when the crucifiers cum they'll fin' an empty tomb.
Now Paul was sich a feller, mos' cruel, hard an' col'.
He'd titles, too, an' honors, an' a cheriot o' gol',
But when he turned he giv' his life fur Him he'd been
    a mockin'—
The bad ain't all in kerriges, nur all the gu'd a-walkin'.

Las' week I saw a workin' man, es po'r es po'r cu'd be,
With nothin' to pay taxes on, except 'twas misery,
Put down his dinner-pail an' turn to cheer an' mil'ly
    chide
A tipsy, broken 'ristocrat who talked o' suicide;
An' yiste'day I saw the man thet po'r mechanic saved,
All shinin' sleek in broadcloth, jes' newly primp'd an'
    shaved,

Go down a muddy alleyway whar' lay a sodden wight,
An' bear him tenderly beyon' the shoutin' rabble's
sight,
An' that is why I'm moved t' say, for all the gloomy
talkin',
The bad ain't all in kerriges, nur all the gu'd a-walking.

So while on one side Selfishness is keepin' what it gets,
An' on the other Envy raves an' curses, fumes an' frets,
Th' quiet people jog along th' road a-tween th' two,
A gettin' gentler all th' time because o' good they do,
A gettin' nearer, nearer yet t' that delightful time
When ev'ry man 'll seek th' true in ev'ry lan' an' clime,
When Ekal Rights 'll compass all the surface o' th'
yearth,
An' man'll rank fur what he is despite o' wealth ur
birth—
Thar won't be any lan'lord then behin' th' tenant
stalkin'
An' gu'd 'll ride on ev'ry side, with Satan, maybe,
walkin'.

A SUMMER PICTURE

In curving silken hammock hung,
She slowly back and forward swung;
Her left hand tost above her head,
And in her right the book she read,
Or seemed to read; yet each white lid,
Blue-veined and heavy fringed, half hid
Her brown-black eyes, whose dreamy light
Shone like a half-seen star at night,
When veil-like mist o'erhangs the air—
And told her thoughts were otherwhere.

Her wealth of yellow tresses caught—
By silver bangles, Venice-wrought—
Back from her brow, full, broad and low
And trackless as new-fallen snow,
Swept sloping downward, wave on wave,
To hide the foam-white shoulders, save
Where, 'twixt dividing, golden strands,
They gleamed like pearls half hid in sands.

One dainty, slippered foot peeped out—
Its arching instep bound about
With narrow bands of black and gold—

From underneath the foam-like fold
Of fluffy gown—greensward beneath,
The trees above a giant wreath;
She seemed not born of earthly strife,
But marble starting into life.

UNDER THE BLOSSOMS

A Mid-May evening, calm, serene;
 The stars assembling faintly smiled
On undulating fields of green,
 On wood where plum and apple wild,
Their every bough a globe of bloom,
 With fragrant odors filled the air,
On stream that in the softened gloom
 Of woodland shade sang sweetly there.

With figure bent and falt'ring pace,
 Up from the vale a pilgrim came;
Pale Want had pinched and limned his face,
 And Sin, Regret and Passion's flame
Had so consumed him that he moved
As one who, having Charon proved,
 Was come again to stroll among
The rich, full beauties of the plain.
 'Twas like a glorious anthem sung,
Wherein is one discordant strain.

Just underneath the blushing bough
 He knelt beside the brook, to cool
His fevered throat and throbbing brow.
 "Dear spot," he murmured, "worse than fool

Was I, to leave so fair a place
  For city's glare and blaze and roar.
O Innocence, thy gentle face
  Shall smile upon me nevermore!"

He paused. Among the tender leaves
  The straying Zephyr sadly sighed.
"And is there any heart that grieves
  Tonight for me?" he sudden cried.
"Ah, God!" At that great word he bowed
  His head until the grasses swept
His sunken cheek, and sobbed aloud,
  And prayer broke from him while he wept.

THE PRAYER.

"Sweet Spirit! Universal All!
  Pure source of gentleness and love!
Who hearest e'en the sparrow call,
  I, to the verge of madness drove,
Hard ridden by a devil horde
  Of scourging fiends, at last to Thee,
Though late, I come; Thou art the Lord—
  Oh, be Thou merciful to me.

"About my head the tempests drive,
  My feet are set in sinking sands,
Within me evils live and thrive,
  To tear the good with cruel hands.

On Virtue I have shut the door;
My heart is lead, O Galilee!
Thy love, Thy favor I implore—
Dear Lord, be merciful to me."

*   *   *   *   *

He slept. Above him sang a thrush;
The twilight deepened into night,
And, in the still and holy hush,
The blossoms, delicately bright,
Came slowly down from branch and bough,
In fragrant clouds came down to hide
The shame of sin and wreck of pride.

They found him there at morning's light,
All wrapped in robes of pink and white—
And peace was on his brow.

THE HAND THAT HOLDS THE PLOW

All about the corn is waving
Emerald green with tips of gold;
Amber wheat-fields sea-like laving
Shores of hedge-row round them roll'd.
'Neath yon poplars tall and stately,
Robed in shimmering silver leaves.
From his farm-house door sedately,
Counts the lord his coming sheaves.
Mark, as evening shadows lengthen,
How he sends delighted eye,
O'er the upland's wealth of treasure,
Where the shaven meadows lie.

  Nature weaves her fairest garlands
  Round the sunburned reaper's brow,
  And the Ship of State is guided
  By the hand that holds the plow.

See his offspring troop about him,
Strong of limb and brown of cheek,
Reared to trust and never doubt him,
Labor taught from week to week.
Within doors the housewife tripping
Back and forth in thoughtful part,
Loving hopes her steps out-stripping,
Born within her mother-heart,

Till the snowy cloth is laden
With the food her hands prepared—
Home-instructed while a maiden—
Richer feast was never shared.
> Nature weaves her fairest garlands
> Round the sunburned reaper's brow,
> And the Ship of State is guided
> By the hand that holds the plow.

Can there grow—in city splendor—
Walled and sunless, rank with sin,
Souls so broad they would defend, or
Die, their country's good to win?
Hero minds need diff'rent feeding—
Hills and valleys, sky and sun,
Such will rise, their country needing,
Rise true patriots every one.
Slavery never can enthrall them,
Gold is serf to Right the king,
Dragon Greed cannot appal them,
Who have heard the river sing.
> Nature weaves her fairest garlands
> Round the sunburned reaper's brow,
> And the Ship of State is guided
> By the hand that holds the plow.

TO A WOUNDED BIRD

Poor little warbler! harmless thing
That late on buoyant, sportive wing,
High up among the clouds, did'st sing
    Thy glad refrain,
Now helpless at my feet you fling,
    The slave of Pain.

Thy voice, that erst, so full and clear,
Was wont my lonely heart to cheer,
Now shrill with pain and piteous fear—
    Cheering no more—
Wins for itself but Pity's tear,
    And grieves me sore.

Poor songster! not thy voice alone
From troubled breast sends up its moan,
Thine not the only pleading tone
    Of breaking heart—
So man must ever sigh and groan
    E'en from the start.

'Tis thus the mortal that has found
Thee, blasted by a cruel wound,
Gropes ever darkly 'round and 'round,
    With mind untaught,
Striving with many a useless bound
    A flight of thought.

So must he ever panting lie,
Far, far below Hope's glowing sky,
To which he fain would quickly fly
    In loving trust,
But ever with a feeble cry
    Falls in the dust.

EASTER LILIES

What though you build cloud-high the wall,
  What though the sword you constant wield!
All kingdoms, monarchies shall fall
Because of these—and over all
  Shall stand the lilies of the field.

BETTER THAN GOLD

Cast your bread upon the water,
  Pleading, hungry at your feet;
High or humble, king or cotter,—
  Charity's returns are sweet.
By a word that's fitly spoken,
  Howe'er simple it may be,
Oft a chain of evil's broken
  And a fettered slave is free.
      Cast your bread upon the waters,
        Tossing sea or dimpled burn,—
      These are all His sons and daughters,—
        Give! nor question the return.

Every tear that's stayed from falling
  Is a diamond for your crown;
O the ceaseless, ceaseless calling
  Of the dear ones trampled down!
But for those whose strength is given
  To the shielding of the weak,
Storms are still, the clouds are riven,
  Zephyrs chant and sunbeams speak.
      Cast your bread upon the waters,
        Frowning sea or dimpled burn—
      These are all His sons and daughters,—
        Give! nor question the return.

Every stream of kindness flowing
  Stays some feet that sin-ward roam;
Every lamp of mercy glowing
  Guides some wand'ring brother home;
Nature opes her veins to nourish
  Vines of truth where'er they run,
And a thousand blossoms flourish,
  Pressing in the track of one.
        Cast your bread upon the waters,
          Moaning sea or dimpled burn—
        These are all His sons and daughters,—
          Give! nor question the return.

Every youth that's upward pointed
  By the riper mind of age,—
Every age by youth anointed,
  Beautifies a barren page.
Patient Faith has ever wrought her
  Triumphs through the gentle heart—
Cast your bread upon the water,
  Heroism's noblest part.
        Cast your bread upon the waters,
          Moaning sea or dimpled burn,
        These are all His sons and daughters,—
          Give! nor question the return.

HE WROTE FOR ALL

"The world is cruel, careless, cold,"
I sighed, "and cares for naught but gold!
Why should my troubled pages plead
A brother's woe—a brother's need!"

"My song is drowned in Mammon's roar,"
(I flung my pen upon the floor)
"The hand that Fortune stoops to bless
Must crush the buds of tenderness."

My toddling wee one put the pen
Into my trembling hand again,
And, clambering upon my knee,
Said, archly: "Papa, wite for me."

I wrote—a homely, childish tale
Of hope and love—no pensive wail
Of others' wrongs—but what her smile
Had wakened in my heart the while.

And when the ink had scarcely dried,
I heard the song on every side;
It filled the land from sea to sea,
While thousands cried, "He wrote for me."

SISTERS OF MERCY

Theirs is the holy beauty that in the lily dwells,
Or sways the purple clover when chime the distant
    bells;
The sweet, unspoken beauty, too delicate to trace,
That hideth in the heart to light the plainest human
    face.

IN RUSSET CLAD

In russet clad, with velvet shoon,
   Sedate and sober,
Symbolical of Life's full noon
   God's answer to the bloom of June-October.

LOVE'S COMPLETENESS

They met 'neath an oak in a sheltered glade,
On a fair May morning,—the bright-eyed maid

And sturdy ploughman—through brown and tan,
Her gaze sank into the soul of the man.

She loved him, and he,—in the fields alone
He lingered wherever a flow'r was blown

To whisper his secret,—the birds all knew,
And sang the story so clear and true

That his great heart thrilled in his bosom grand,
Lest others should hear them and understand.

They met, and there at the maiden's feet,
A wild rose nestled secure and sweet.

He plucked the blossom with tender care,
And twining the stem in her golden hair,

Low whispered: " 'Tis crowned with a gem of dew,
It shall gleam in your tresses, a crown for you,

The queen of all flow'rs, from the violet
That looks from your eyes, to the blooms which fret

The boughs of the oak where the woodbine clings,
And the wild dove nests and the red-bird sings.

Then down from a branch, as he tremulous spoke,
Slow drifted a leaf from the listening oak,—

Till swaying and shifting, like mystical wand,
It rested at last in the maiden's hand.

Quickly she clasped it, to answer him—"See!
The oak of the forest is most like thee.

From your lips come words, as the leaves that fall,
That are rich with comfort and cheer for all.

The tree to the hurricane offers its breast,
That the weak in its bosom may shelter and rest,

It broadens its shade in the noontide heat,
And peaceful comfort envelops its feet.

The modest blossom that decks my braid
Came fearless forth in its cooling shade.

Nay, look where the trunk by the storm is riven,
To the weaker vines is a foothold given,

And mount they gaily in loving strife,
To broader and sweeter and sunnier life.

Though man may harshly these faults condemn,
They are rounds in the ladder of hope to them.

The flower is fragile, but strong the tree,
The oak for you, and the rose for me.

Spring went and came with its bud and bloom,
With sunshine and song and the flash of plume.

The rich full Autumn turned gold and red
The great green wreath 'round the old oak's head,

But ever again when the soft May air
Is kissing the lips of the roses fair,

In the quiet shade of the oak, these twain
That glad spring morning live over again.

And youthful faces about them bend,
And youthful voices in harmony blend.

There are tongues a-prattle and pattering feet,
The oak, the rose with the vines complete.

FORSAKEN

O shadow of Erebus, hide me;
   The day hath no pleasure for me.
Nor human nor angel may guide me;
   I drift on an under-world sea,
Shut in by the Mountain of Reason,
   Storm-beaten by Reason's disdain—
A cycle declined to a season,
   An unbroken winter of pain.

Shut in by a custom unshaken,
   Shut out from the sweetness of home;
From visions of joy I awaken,
   To battle with demon and gnome.
My soul as a bird of the morning,
   Went soaring and singing thy name;
Now, stripped for thy selfish adorning,
   It creeps back in darkness and shame.

The hands that so gently caress thee
   Hold lashes to scourge me; the lips
That trouble sweet heaven to bless thee
   Curse me to the verge of eclipse.
God pity them, dearest! God pity!
   For myself, I shall finish the jest
With a meaningless laugh through the city,
   To sleep in the River of Rest.

THE BETTER YEAR

Two radiant stars in the long ago
  Shone fair on a world with the war aflame,
And men grew gentler for Sappho's woe,
  And nobler because of a Roman's fame.

Yet brute-blood lingered, and nobles heard
  The shriek of anguish without a sigh,
And the veins of matron and maiden stirred
  And thrilled with pleasure to see men die.

How pale thy passion, O singer sweet!
  How dim thy glory, O man of pride!
In the love-light born where the two worlds meet,
  At the tomb of the Nazarene, crucified!

Are hands still crimson with life's dear bloom?
  Does love still bleed in the press of strife?
Do sun-beams struggle through clouds of gloom
  That rise from the furnace of sordid life?

Behold the selfish turned strangely just,
  The just grown gentle; the kind, sincere!
While fruit displaces the hardened crust
  In the softened glow of a better year.

THE OUTCASTS

High in an attic, grim and scant,
  A ragged creature lonely sat—
His face was limned with pain and want;
At once he cried, "Begone! Avaunt!"
  As o'er the threshold crept a cat.

"Stay, stranger, do not drive me hence?
  I pray thee, list my tale of woe,
I am too poor to give offense,
And stripped of every finer sense,
  I scarce fear either word or blow.

"It was not always so; before
  They turned me out the streets to roam,
I always found an open door.
Alas, when we grow old and poor,
  That we should be without a home!

"The children loved to stroke my back,
  When I was sleek, and round, and fat—
Watch the sparks fly and hear them crack,
And call me pretty puss. Alack,
  I'm now but a neglected cat!

"Once, when a bell the children found—
   A tiny, tinkling bell—they tied
It with a pretty ribbon round
My throat, and at its merry sound
   They laughed and laughed until they cried.

"But now whene'er my form they spy
   With ready hand they fling the bat,
And I am forced for life to fly;
I've lost a foot—an ear—an eye:
   Alas, I am a sorry cat!"

"Poor creature, you have come at last,
   To one who feels your woe—like you,
By all the harsh, cold world outcast,
To dream of an embittered past
   That proved all false he once deemed true.

"Come, outcast, ragged as you are,
   Take half my crust: 'tis hard and dry,
And all I have—but you shall share;
And, while I live, so shall you fare
   Till one or both of us shall die."

SNOW VIOLETS

O bravely the violets bloom in the snow:
The chill winds of March that are hurrying so
Seem tempted to linger—regretfully go
From the fragrant sweet violets sprung from the
snow.

Man's work, not his strength, but his weakness re-
veals:
O'er drunken with knowledge humanity reels
By the fountains of wisdom. The lowliest flower
Surpasses the wonderful: castle and tower,
Carved marble, oiled canvas, how poorly they show
Where the brave little violets bloom in the snow.

THE FALSE NOTE

Does a strain of exultation
  Steal, unbidden, to the tone
Voicing sympathy and comfort,
  When another's hope is flown?
Does regret come slyly plucking
  At the sleeve, while we rejoice
When another has succeeded
  By his deed, or pen, or voice?
Hail the blemish in the blossom!
  Hail the discord in the tune!
We should come to hate the roses
  Were the year a round of June.

SUB ROSA

So small a thing as one wee kiss;
You surely won't refuse me this?
From all your store, you'll never miss—
There! Tell me, Bright-eyes, tell me true,
You rather like it? Yes, you do!

Is there a bee from such a flower
Would flee till drunken in the bower?
How? No, this is the quiet hour;
We're unobserved. What if who knew?
Oh, so you like it? Yes, you do!

He who should kiss and tell, must be
Still more devoid of heart than he
Who scorns to kiss at all. And see,
Now that you're certain I'll be true,
For each I give I get back two.

ETERNITY

Go where the tow'ring precipice
  Frowns on the climbing sea;
Go where the air is frightened by
  Niagria leaping free;
Go where the hungry-featured crowd
  About the custom-place,
Their fingers white with clutching tight
  The curse of Adam's race—
And then at quiet hour of night
  Go muse upon the stars
That fret the sweeping arch of heav'n
  With all their countless bars,
And know that when this heaving mass
  Is fallen to decay,
Those stars will shine serenely on
  And on and on alway.

AN APRIL EVENING.

The virgin leaves in friendly play,
The thrush a-tremble with his lay,
  The snipe's dull boom, the plover's call,
  The robin's treble winding through it all.

ON AN OLD DOOR-STONE AT YALE

What devious paths they since have trod,
  The feet that wore this granite thin;
But leveled forest, broken sod
And temples leaping up to God
  Tell where their ways have been.

THE POET

A poet is—why, naught but this:
A throbbing instrument, whose strain,
When joyous, is most full of pain,
When mournful, rich in bliss.
A fettered bird that longs to fly,
Yet, freed, droops nerveless, idly by,
Nor spreads its wings till, chain'd once more,
It beats its life out in a vain attempt to soar.

A poet is—why, who can tell?
Companion of sweet Nature's joy,
Fate's idle plaything, Passion's toy,
Combined of Heaven and Hell.
He pores above the Book of Man,
Its close-writ pages each to scan,
Learns every thought to feel and state,
And rides o'er darkling cares and woes elate.

This is a poet; more than this,
He knows the grandeur heroes feel
When surging on with naked steel
Where death's hot missiles hiss;
With them he scales the battlements
Through battle-smoke and carnage dense,
With blood-dyed blade and batter'd shield,
Till waves their flag triumphant o'er the field,

This is the poet, ay! and more;
His fate it is to hold and bound
A soul that, like a sea of sound,
Breaks on a farthest shore.
Through darkness of the lengthened night
To labor with a Heav'n-born might
Distilling dewdrops, pure and clear,
That diamond-like touch up the wordly ear.

'TIS NOBLE TO LABOR

'Tis noble to labor, but low to slave,
We should cleave our task as the ship the wave,
Not falter and flounder, as through a wood
Grown rank with briars; half understood
The thing appals us; well learned it seems
As smoothly pleasant as childhood's dreams.
We joy in the progress each day we make,
And labor is sweet for its own dear sake.

The nigardly miser we may despise,
But rational saving is good and wise;
The independent is he who can
Grant favors, nor ask them of any man.
What pleasure the poor to assist, but when
The needy are those whom we love; ah then
The clink of silver and gold's bright shine
Bring joy to the giver that's quite divine.

I KNOW

I know that joy is everywhere,
  That trooping pleasures fill the earth,
For all day long before my door
  The children sport in noisy mirth.

I know that Charity is queen,
  And kindness leavens more and more,
For gates are open in the wall
  That once divided rich and poor.

I am not wise to answer those
  Who call me mad, but this I know,
That all the world is leal and true,
  Because the ones I love are so.

AN AUTUMN TRAGEDY

Mid-afternoon. All overhead
  A trackless, blue expanse,
Along the stream the sumac red
  Defiant rears his lance.
The partridge in the hollows drum,
  The bannered maples gleam,
And naked cotton-wood and plum
  Hang ghostly o'er the stream.

The spring brook, through an avenue
  Of yellowed beach and elm,
Bears gayly on, with ants for crew—
  A cricket at the helm—
A broad, frost-curled, catalpa leaf,
  Its prow with silver crossed—
Two pebbles form a deadly reef,
  The shipwrecked crew is lost.

HOPE

When the weight of sorrow presses on the weary,
  weary heart;
When the future we have trusted fails to do its promised part
As it sweeps into the present—when we shrink, de-
  ceived, betrayed,
With the fruit of Expectation turning bitter in the
  shade
Of the Tree of Knowledge reaching, with its one for-
  bidden bough,
Through the shadow of the ages to the stern and star-
  ing now;
When the long-desired fulfillment, clasped at last in our
  embrace,
Proves a chill and bloodless nothing with a stolid,
  painted face;
When the sinking sky is darkened with the gloomings
  of despair,
Not a single star to brighten—only blackness every-
  where—
Comes a breeze so gently blowing, comes a warm and
  tender light,
Stealing up the eastern heaven, and Despair and sable
  Night
Slowly fade away together—Morning trips along the
  slope,
And the spirit's day breaks newly with the dawning
  light of Hope.

A LEGEND OF ESQUIMAU BAY

O bright was the morning! All nature adorning,
  The sunbeams of summer shone free,
When Mary came down o'er the sands from the town
  To the damp golden rim o' the sea.

For her Jamie today would go sailing away,
  To a country is strange to her ken,
And through a whole year she must sorrow and fear
  And wait for his coming again.

Now she reaches the dock—in his blue sailor smock
  A gay ribboned cap on his head,
With his hands stretchin' out—there be men all about,
  But she falls in his arms like the dead.

The face now at rest on his high-heaving breast,
  It is white as the April day snow;
Jamie sobs out a cry: "Help men, she will die!"
  As gently he sways to and fro.

And the twice helpless men mutter over again,
  "Et will die, pretty lass, thet et will!"
And down the rough cheeks of each one as he speaks
  Flows many a heart-touching rill.

But they stand like a ship that is moored in the slip,
  With hearts, but no knowledge to do,
Till at last Mary sighs, slowly opens her eyes,
  And looks round on the pitying crew.

Then the blood to her face comes in hurrying race,
  As she hides her wet cheeks on the breast
Of Jamie, while they to a man turn away
  And point to the sea's foaming crest.

The farewells are passed, and the good ship at last
  Has sailed from the sheltering quay,
And wringing her hands Mary comes o'er the sands,
  Her face turning still to the sea.

A year has gone by, and the summer draws nigh,
  The sunlight is warm on the bay,
But no other ship's been where the good ship was seen
  That bore the brave sailor away.

The night it was dark and the tempest blew stark
  With the mad waters pounding the shore,
"Mither, list!" Mary said, as she turned in her bed,
  "There's some un wha knocks at the door.

"Ther's some 'un wha knocks an a ship on the rocks,
  I can hear, mither, breakin' her sides!"
"T'sleep, child, nae fear, 'tis the winds that y' hear
  And the high rollin' sweep o' the tides!"

"There's some 'un wha calls, mither, some 'un wha calls,
　It is Jamie's voice, mither, I know!"
"Na, child, dinna min', 'tis the gale in the pine
　'Et lifts on the crag there below!"

The tempest grew still as she spoke, on the sill
　A half-sound of hurrying feet,
The barred door swung wide, and with still, ghostly
　　stride
　Came Jamie, his Mary to greet.

His face was as grave as the curve of a wave,
　The seaweed was wound in his hair,
His jacket was gray with the sand and the spray,
　And the sea-brine that dripped from it there.

The mother grew white and still with affright,
　But Mary sighed, "Jamie, 'tis he!"
No word Jamie spake, but her hands he did take
　And pointed away to the sea.

Her eyes to his own all so trustfully shone,
　While slowly she rose from the bed,
And with him she passed through the door—holding
　　fast
　To the hand of the wraith of her dead.

Again the storm grew, louder yet the winds blew,
　The door slowly swung to its place—
And in shivering fright the poor mother all night
　Cowered there with close covered face.

The morning came fair with a soft gentle air,
　But sorrow was over the town,
For the good ship Labrocks on the sharp cruel rocks,
　In the storm of the night had gone down.

And there were a score of brave men or more
　That the waves to the shallows had borne;
And many a Kate must weep for her mate
　And many a mother must mourn.

Where Mary had dwelt the poor mother knelt
　In a corner with meaningless stare,
"Christ, Jesu!" cried she, pointing out to the sea,
　"My Mary and Jamie are there."

Now by Esquimau Bay, so the village folk say,
　When at night the storm lashes the sea,
Their wraiths hand in hand may be seen on the strand
　As loving as lovers may be.

WISDOM

Wouldst thou gather wisdom? Go
Where the gentle waters flow,
Where the flowers and the trees
Sway in converse with the breeze;
Where around the mountain's poll
Silence thunders to the soul.
Mysteries from two concealed
Oft to him are clear revealed
Who, in solitude, alone.
Lingers where a flow'r is blown,
Feels the music, as it passes,
Of the marshal-hearted grasses
Pressing forward out of night
Into liberty and light.
Forth in evening's calm, to view
Heav'n's star-lighted vault of blue;
Note the bull-bat's noiseless flight
Through the silver gray of night;
List the crickets piping slip
From the clover; watch the dip
Of the sword of Dian, prest
Slow into the mountain's breast,
Where he rears him, stern and grim,
On the Occidental rim.
Knowledge weaves of earthly things,
Wisdom mounts on eagle wings,
Wins the Parcae's magic wand,
And peers into the world's beyond.

MAY

We heard not a sound of their marshaling feet,
Saw never the gleam of a spear,
Till their tents stood saucily fronting each street,
And the army of blossoms is here.

MARCH

Pale autumn moves, with gentle tread
And quiet air, among the dead;
March whips the sullen sky to tears,
And lo! the violet appears.

A MORNING SPIN.

Again I mount to whirl along
    The singing breeze,
(The world hath not another song
    So like to please!)
By hedges green, through leafy wood,
    O'er meadow wide,
A joy-compelling Robin Hood,
    I noiseless glide.

Yon swallow sailing through the sky
    Hath greater need
Of man's companionship than I
    Upon this steed.

What fragrant odors where I run,
    And merry chimes,
And songs (O sweet unworded one
    Of mellow rhymes!)
Embow'ring trees, the waving corn,
    Gay winding brook,
And dew drops flashing to the morn
    Where e'er I look.

Yon swallow sailing through the sky
    Hath greater need
Of man's companionship than I
    Upon this steed.

O wond'rous offspring of the mind!
   O precious prize!
Thou bear'st me swifter than the wind
   'Neath smiling skies.
Half drunken with the joy I feel,
   Sweet Zephyr-fanned,
A conquerer of time I reel
   Through fairy land.

Yon swallow sailing through the sky
   Hath greater need
Of man's companionship than I
   Upon this steed.

HANDSOMEST OF ALL

True, you may not call her handsome—
  May not even deem her fair;
In her cheeks no roses blossom;
  Gold-gleams flash not in her hair;
Smoother brows there are, and whiter,
  Eyes that hold a gayer light—
Neither are her finger's taper
  Nor her hands as lilies white;
In her step there's nothing fawn-like,
  Low and tremulous her tones—
But far dearer her possessions,
  Sweeter still the charm she owns.
There are others worth admiring,
  Handsome if you will—but she
Is my mother, tender, loving,
  Handsomest of all to me.

'Round her brow there winds a garland
  Of a thousand answered prayers;
In her hand she bears the lilies
  Of a thousand lightened cares;
Every tress that Time has silvered
  By an angel's kiss is blest;
And her cheeks have burned their roses
  On the love-fires in her breast.
With the strength her toils have wasted

Manly hearts beat high today,
  Storing for her future comfort,
    Pouring gladness in her way.
There are others worth admiring,
  Handsome if you will—but she
Is my mother—tender, loving,
  Handsomest of all to me.

In this gentle, trustful clinging
  I can read the far-off past—
See myself as timid, falt'ring,
  To her firmness anchored fast.
How she soothed each childish sorrow,
  Smoothed each wrinkle from my brow,
Kissed away the tears and cheered me,
  Even as I cheer her now.
Life is but a half-spelled sentence
  Scattered o'er a blotted page,
But the heart that's true remembers
  Age is youth and youth is age.
There are others worth admiring,
  Handsome if you will—but she
Is my mother—tender, loving,
  Handsomest of all to me.

There are loves and loves in plenty
  Which to win I oft am fain,
Rich as skies of autumn morning,
  Warm as sunshine after rain;

But their shining is as shadow,
  And their warmth, compared to hers
Is as loosely woven laces
  To the soft New Zealand furs;
Often hath my heart a yearning
  Nothing will assuage but this,
Her dear fingers on my forehead,
  On my lips her holy kiss.
And when round His throne we gather,
  Of all saints she still will be
Fairest, purest, dearest, sweetest,
  Handsomest of all to me.

EPISTLE TO OPIE READ

Hail! goddess of the yellow braid!
The Queen of press and measure!
Now are the rural toils repaid
With heaps of shining treasure.

Ye desk-worn! throw your pens aside,
  Discard the puzzling book,
And come where skies are blue and wide,
  And thought is like the brook
That sings along the hazel slope
  And leaps among the rocks.
The woods! The fields! Renew your hope,
  And the luster in your locks!

Come where the salmon graceful glide,
  Their golden sides a-quiver—
Or where the stubborn pike divide
  The swiftly flowing river.
Come where the partridge-thunder peals,
  Aud mallards part the rushes
As o'er the bridge, with creaking wheels,
  The loaded wagon crushes.

Come where the quail prophetic speaks,
  And where the saffron boughs
The playful jay with sapphire streaks;
  Come where the hungry plows

Devour the stubble, flashing bright
   At every turn; and swains
Who strip the golden ears delight
   The fields with jocund strains.

Along the stream the peaceful kine
   Industrious crop the heath—
Their full distended bellies shine,
   Their glossy sides beneath,
While round the sullen monarch glow'rs,
   His front all-sable curled,
With mutt'rings fierce proclaims his pow'rs.
   Then challenges the world.

My friend, to your creative mind
   These scenes I know are dear,
For them your converse I resigned,
   For you I sing them here;
Nor do all rural subjects bear
   The rude untutored part,
Full oft the shy reserve they wear
   Conceals a trusty heart.

Where blossoms 'broider every path,
   And climbing roses grace
The cottage doorway, Spite and Wrath
   Find thorny resting-place.
Here e'en the ever-boding crow
   Croaks in a smoother way,
And blackbirds seem each noon to know
   A still more tuneful lay.

At early morn to meet the sun
  My joyful way I take—
How musical the brooks that run
  To leap into the lake!
The timid plovers veering rise
  With supplicating cry—
The pointed pinion swiftly plies
  Along the purpling sky.

Now fair amidst his shining force
  The God of day appears.
Swift up the sky he holds his course;
  Speed forth the gleaming spears,
Till every dusky shape is slain
  That steads the courts of night,
And swims the woodland, hill and plain,
  In warm, refulgent light.

When midway in the tender blue
  The sun all shadows cheer,
I seek the wood and there review
  The books of Hope and Fear,
The hoarding squirrel shrilly calls,
  "The winter comes; lay by!"
"Enjoy," cries every leaf that falls,
  "Decay and death are nigh."

The gray dove now, forsaken bird,
  Bemoans its absent mate;
Now winds the heavy-uddered herd
  Slow through the pasture gate.

The careful herdsman stands to count,
　And ere his task be done,
High up the rocky ledge I mount
　To view the setting sun.

The budding Spring is gay with song.
　The summer boasts her charms,
And when old Winter roars along
　How grand are his alarms!
But Autumn! Life's dividing line—
　The round year's richest part!
You've many an abler pen than mine,
　But no more faithful heart.

LOU M. WILSON

Art weary, love, despondent, weak?
  Look up! the skies are thine;
What though today be cold and bleak,
  The morrow's sun will shine.
Come, take my hand, 'tis firm and strong,
  'Twill give you hope and cheer—
What though the way be dark and long,
  If so that Love be near?

Look forward—never backward—heart,
  The past comes not again.
The sunbeams on the mountain dart
  Though clouds o'erhang the plain.
Up higher yet! The risk is great?
  The prize is what you will;
The faithful sing at Heaven's gate,
  The indolent are still.

THE HORSE-SHOE BADGE

How pleasing the strains of the harp or piano,
How stirring the call of the bugle or drum;   ·
And hopeful the song of the robin in spring-time,
When trees are a-bud and the violets come;
How dreamful the sound of the rain on the clover,
In stillness that follows Jove's threatening roll;
But the music that hurries my blood and awakens
The sweetest and holiest chords in my soul,
　　Is the chink, chink, chink,
　　And the clink, clink, clink,
Where the forge-flame ebbs and flows.
　　And I pause whene'er
　　On the air I hear
The ring of the blacksmith's blows,
As he turns the shoe in whose form I see
The symbol of all that is dear to me.

Now firmly the links of affection are welded,
I know those again I had not thought to know;
O, peace of the soul and a constant sweet quiet,
Beyond all the power of the craftiest foe
To darken or trouble or hinder or ruffle;
Not sighing of Sappho, or piping of Pan,
Hold half so sweet measure to stir me or thrill me,
As the strokes of this brawny-armed, soot-powdered
　　man,

With his chink, chink, chink,
And his clink, clink, clink,
Where the forge-flame ebbs and flows,
And I pause whene'er
On, the air I hear
The ring of the blacksmith's blows,
As he turns the shoe in whose form I see
The symbol of all that is dear to me.

WHITTIER

I saw the moaning ocean turn
  To leave the weeping land,
And then come laughing back again,
  A white wreath in its hand.

I saw the full moon creep behind
  A cloud that hid its light,
To re-appear high up above,
  A hundred-fold more bright.

I saw a herdsman lead afar
  His panting, thirsty flocks,
I saw the waters burst for him
  In fullness from the rocks.

I saw the negro scourged and bound,
  I heard the hammer fall,
And then the Nation's mighty voice:
  "Be free, my children, all!"

He trod where only prophets tread;
  Put these sad symbols by,
And bring them forth when one is dead—
  And Whittier cannot die.

GRANT—A REQUIEM

Though Sierra's crags enfold me
  Where tonight I sit alone;
Though no human tongue hath told me,
  Yet I know that he is gone.

For the winds that erst were sighing
  In the swaying boughs o'erhead,
"He is dying! He is dying!"
  Now are moaning, "He is dead!"

Till the clouds, symphonious roaring,
  Clasp the shiv'ring mountain round,
Deep into the canyons pouring
  Monodies of mournful sound.

Quick, recurrent fires go reeling
  Through the sable skies and light
Earth's tumultuous breast, revealing
  All the storm's majestic might.

And behold; with aspect solemn,
  High above, the god of war
Leading forth an endless column
  Toward th' one unclouded star.

Soldier spirits long have slumbered,
  Deaf to bugle, fife and drum,
Waiting in their graves unnumbered,
  Waiting till the chief should come.

On they sweep, a line unbroken,
  Through the sky with steady tread—
Though no human tongue hath spoken,
  Thus I know that Grant is dead.

SOLITUDE

The black-winged tempest of the night
  Its wrathful course had run,
And, like a tired child, the sea
  Slept in the noon-day sun.

Far shoreward stretched the moor-lands wide,
  Marked by a single oak—
The Storm King's fiery saber smote
  And killed it at a stroke.

A barren beach swept to the right
  In long, low-swirling drifts,
While gray and cold upon the left
  Uprose the beetling cliffs.

Before the sea so hushed and still,
  It only moved to sigh,
And overhead the boundless blue
  Of an unclouded sky.

The mellow sunlight on the land,
  The sunlight on the wave.
The sea a-beat against the cliff
  Like Love against a grave.

On jutting crag a fish-hawk plumed
  His steel-blue, glassy coat,
Then headlong plunged into the wave,
  The death-cry in his throat,—

A cry that echoed far and wide;
  But one who soundly slept
Where shelving beach and waters met,
  Unbroken silence kept.

The sunlight in her clinging robe,
  The sunlight in her hair,
The waters lisping at her feet
  Held all of life was there.

No eye to weep, no voice to mourn,
  No touch of loving hand;
All waxen-white and still she lay
  Alone upon the sand.

The timid Zephyr nearer crept,
  And one, more kind and bold,
Upraised her hair and vailed her face
  With half its wealth of gold.

Alone she lay who yesterday
  Was half a city's pride,
The queen of speechless solitude
  And desolation's bride.

THE SIRE OF EIGHT

A lonely bachelor I came
　　Where homelike gardens fringed the town,
And by a cozy hearthstone flame
　　With loving friend I sat me down.

Not forty, and eight times a sire,
　　Nor forty, and nine voices sweet
The blessed morning hymn to choir,
　　The evening coming-home to greet.

Four clinging girls, four sturdy boys,
　　Each dearer than the Ophir mine,
Not forty, and prospective joys
　　Already multiplied by nine.

The rose that bends beside his door,
　　While but a single rose to me,
Ten times for him it blooms and fades,
　　Ere drifting to th' Eternal Sea.

Ten hearts to throb with one's success,
　　Ten heads to bow with grief of one;
Oh, blessed wealth of tenderness!
　　Oh, awful poverty of none!

Some lives are like a riven drum,
　Some glad as nesting robbin's mate—
A lonely bachelor I come,
　To sit beside the sire of eight.

JOHN ALBRO

He found my muse—a wayward child,
　In pleasure romping where she would;
A free-limbed daughter of the wild,
　Sans ribbon, bodice, shoon or hood,
And led her by persuasive art
　To quiet ways and comely gown—
Until (the wild-wood in her heart)
　She moves demurely in the town.

CHRISTMAS EVE AT THE OLD HOMESTEAD

From low-hung clouds of leaden gray
    The fluffy flakes came down
Till every shrub and bush was gay
    In bridal wreath and gown;
What time the moon, of gibbous form,
    Clear in the heaven stood
Above the farm-house, sheltered warm
    By the embow'ring wood.

About the valley, lily fair,
    The hills voluptuous swell,
A lonely poplar here and there
    Keeps jealous sentinel;
The spring brook, with a merry smile,
    Flings in old Winter's face,
Then gaily glints beyond the stile
    And skips his cold embrace.

The old folk by the chimney nook
    Think on the ones who roam,
And lamps from every window look
    To light the absent home;
Home! where they first, wee toddlers, crept
    Along the oaken floor,
Where childhood laughed till manhood wept
    A parting at the door.

Of all the brood but one remains
  To cheer the parent nest,
Support their age and soothe their pains—
  The youngest, dearest, best
Of all the precious, treasured seven
  Who in their hearts abide—
Though some are here and some in heaven—
  God keep him by their side.

They come! The venerable pair,
  With kisses, tears and smiles,
Give welcome to the strong and fair
  Who've scorned dividing miles
To meet beneath the homestead roof;
  Grandchildren trooping round
In noisy play, without reproof,
  Make all the house resound.

Now sinks the memory of care
  In Pleasure's golden sea;
If Ned and Bess their favors share
  In shadow, where can be
The harm? Shall cousins never kiss?
  The game of forfeits, ho!
Decorum! such an hour as this
  Rules her its mortal foe.

Five-summer Edna fairy tales
  With cousin Ralph would share;
Maturely eight, his soul regales
  Itself on giant fare,

Which Dick and Bird, ancients of ten,
  Demurely smile to hear,
Half wishing they were young again
  To hold such trifles dear.

But when the sturdy Welshman Ben,
  By years of service proved,
Brings in a log two modern men
  Not easily had moved,
And flings it crashing to the flames,
  Each to the chimney hies
And hastily an ember names
  To watch it till it dies.

Thus Yuletide hours all gaily fly
  Away on swallow wings,
The merry laughter, swelling high,
  Is hushed as midnight rings;
And round the fire, in varied groups,
  Are hung the chubby hose;
Good-night! and hopeful childhood troops
  To innocent repose.

O childhood! sinless as the flakes
  That kiss the clouds good-by!
The memory of thee awakes
  The suppliant's dearest sigh;
And wore I here a monarch's crown
  Above these thinning locks,
How gladly would I cast it down
  To be a child in frocks.

FATHER DAMIEN

I stand uncovered by a grave
  Wherein a hero molds;
Yet never battle-axe nor stave
His hand embraced, nor weapon, save
  The touch that kindness holds.

No sculptured column marks the place,
  But here by weeds o'ergrown,
With patient care I faintly trace,
"The savior of our stricken race."
  Carved in a cross of stone.

What loving fingers held the knife
  That spelled this ragged line?
Though they had every soil to wife
I'd give a twelvemonth of my life
  To clasp them once in mine.

For one beneath this ivy sleeps
  The world shall longer know
Than any name the New World keeps,
Than any e'er from Alpine steeps
  Rang o'er a conquered foe.

His acts pales all heroic deeds
  Though Homers twenty sung them;
The isle Unclean! Alas the needs
Of those on whom that vampire feeds!
  Serene he moved among them,

And braved a death which e'en in thought
  Appalls our every sense;
Day after day in patience wrought
For those whose lightest touch is fraught
  With woeful pestilence.

The blue-rimmed ocean shut him in
  From all his nobler kind;
Abandoned in that Isle of Sin,
By horrors haunted, there to win
  To hope the hopeless mind.

The ships that sailed in silence by
  Must e'er anew have stirred
The memories which could not die,
The joys of home, love's tender sigh,
  The greeting smile and word.

There could he sit with trusty friends
  At close of winter day,
And join the cheer that converse lends
To social mirth when wisdom bends
  To wit's delightful play—

If so he dreamed none ever knew;
  The ties of earth were riven—
Priest, brother, nurse, he loved and drew
His charge to love him and renew
  Their faith and hope in Heaven.

No marble marks his resting place,
  By ivy overgrown;
But here with patient care I trace,
"The savior of our stricken race,"
  Cut in a cross of stone.

M'CULLOUGH

Grand as the eagle in soaring flight
  Sweeping the mountain's brow;
Grand as Ocean when storm-mad night
Hurls wave on wave till they're crested white;
Grand as the prairie whose boundless sweep
Is giant rhythm, or still as sleep
  On the brow of death. What pow'r hadst thou
To wake our frenzy or win our tears!
  "Virginia! Virginia!" I hear thee now,
Though still thy voice as the Roman years.

JAMES

Name's Jim, Jim Burke.
Am I lookin' fur work?
Can't say et' I am,
Ain't much uv a lamb—
Got any employ?
Don't want it, old boy,
Leastwise not now—
How?
Sit down, ye shall hear—
Ho, waiter, s'm beer—
Can ye see in the shade
The mark 'et uz made
By the ball an' chain?—
The Gov'ment rein
'S been drawed on me
An' ye must agree
'T thar's reason enough
Why I should be tough
But none et all
Why I should crawl
In the wake uv a clown,
My back bowed down
By a load o' brick,—
I'd do et 'an quick
But whar's the use;
I kin stan' abuse

A durned sight better when et's
    deserved.
Uv course, I hev served
Time,
Not in this clime,
But the mark is heie,
Burned deep. Mebbe queer,
But you are the fust—
Here waiter's your dust,—
What'll ye have? Don't drink?
Well, here's what I think
O' you 'ristocrat bloods
With yer trim-cut duds
An' yer milk-sop ways,
I would smash y' all
As I smash this glass—
H'm, let that pass.
Good? away back thar—
If y' knew o' the load
'Et a man must bear
Who starts in the world
Like a sail half furled,
'Thout perfession ur trade:—
Hev ye heard the sound that is
    sometimes made
By the wind in the trees
    when the leaves is wet?
If ye have, I'll bet
The whole o' my kit
That ye can't fergit

How it kind o' softened your heart
     an' set
Yer mind on the days o' the
     apple bloom
An' the woods an' the brook an'
     the partridge boom,
An' the wild strawberry hid deep in
     the grass,—
What's that! did my elbow push
     that glass
To the floor?
Let it lie
I
Ain't usin' the stuff no more.
D'ye hear!
No, keep your talk.
Let's walk,
An' you may introduce me to your
     work,
Me, Jim Burke.
The same's
From this time for'ard t' be called James.

THE MAESTRO

In bare, uncurtained room he sat,
An old man, hollow-eyed and thin,
And listless stroked his violin.

From country lane a vagrant breeze
Came by and tossed into the room
The fragrance of the clover bloom.

With flashing eye and shaking mane,
He stood erect a king of kings—
His bow had touched the sleeping strings.

KEELEY

Close reef that name, each added title trim,
What matter titles to a man like him!
The thing he did and not the words he said
Will move a world to weep him when he's dead.

THE BATTERED OLD GRIP

(Respectfully dedicated to Mr. Brenton R. Wells.)

Dear comrade, once bright as the silk of the corn,
Now shrunken and wrinkled, a subject of scorn,
Your trappings, once brilliant, now tarnished and
     scaled,
The key long since lost and every clasp failed,
Your sides fallen inward in gaunt hungry way,
And rich russet color, dull, faded and gray;
Ah! lightly through aisles of my memory trip
A troop of bright fancies at sight of my "grip."

Preparing to start on a journey, how oft
I have taken it down from its place in the loft,
Spread it wide at my feet with its back to the floor,
With the thought—Will it hold all my things as be-
     fore?
Friends tried often prove quite as cruel as kind,
For words like to thistledown drift with the wind;
But here's a companion ne'er gave me the slip—
Always faithful and willing my battered old "grip."

First a half-dozen shirts seem to fill up each side,
Yet kerchiefs a dozen, scarfs tied and untied,
Pipe, razor and strop, cuffs, collars and gloves,
With a score of small knick-knacks tucked into the
     grooves;
A clothes brush, pomade, a picture or two

Of a dear little lassie to look at when blue,
And mayhap a small phial containing a "nip."
All snugly pack into the battered old grip.

The great ocean steamer, with cabin and hold,
Hangs the sign out at last "No more here enrolled,"
The street-car, capacity something immense—
May sometimes refuse you a place for your pence;
E'en the venerable stage, despite legend and lore,
Not always can proffer the "room for one more,"
Yet truth has deserted the heart and the lip
Of him who should say, "No more room in the grip."

Slow out from the shadow sweet memories drift
Through th' channels of thought—and its worn form
    I lift
With a reverent touch while I think, with a sigh,
Of the many dear treasures, in days are gone by,
That have lain in its pockets and hid in its depths— .
A mother's admonishings, father's precepts,
And others with token from maiden's pure lip,
Read over and over—held place in the "grip."

Though my hair is beginning to silver, I feel
A rapturous youthfulness over me steal
As I gaze at these dingy old covers and think,
In my first manhood days, how I stood on the brink
Of life's speeding river, and dreamed of and plann'd
A home just the neatest and best in the land,
Where a sweet face should greet me, returned from
    each trip,
With a welcoming smile for myself and the "grip."

God bless every stitch in the shrunken old leather
That's borne me in safety through all kinds of
     weather
To this island of peace which I now so enjoy,
With my dear little wife, my girl and my boy!
God bless it, I say, and in palace or cot,
In wealth or in poverty—whate'er my lot—
Though Fate from my savings all other things strip,
I'll cling to you ever, dear battered old "grip."

THE OLDEST O' THEM ALL

You may see him any evening sitting just outside the
   door
Of a pretty rural cottage that the vines have clam-
   bered o'er,
And the pink and cherry blossoms slyly peep about
   him there,
Like so many fairies playing hide-and-seek behind
   his chair.
He's a lean and slippered figure and his step is far
   from light,
There are furrows in his forehead and his hair is
   snowy white
And his cheeks, like aged parchment, yellow, wrinkled, worn and grim—
Yet not a drummer of them all but doffs the hat to
   him.

He can sing (his voice will quaver) songs forgotten
   long ago.
By the present generation, songs our fathers used
   to know,
And their rhythm quaint reminds you of a brook
   and falling leaves,
And a maple-shadowed cottage with the swallows
   'neath the eaves.
Then he'll tell you of adventures that will thrill your
   heart with fear,
Or recount a world of stories you will laugh for
   hours to hear,

While his eyes anew will sparkle 'neath his hat's ex-
    tended rim—
There's not a drummer in the land but yields the
    palm to him.

How his withered form will straighten as he "reck-
    ons" in his day
"Thar wusn't many ov um," when he felt inclin'd
    that way,
"Wi the peart and smilin' lassies" that he met along
    the "raout,"
If he chose to show his samples "as could lay th'
    old man aout."
He will call to mind the stage-coach with its flyers,
    six or more,
"Faster than y're modern engines wi' their smoke an'
    dust an' roar
Sweepin' round' the yawning canyons lighter than the
    swallows skim—"
Oh! not a drummer in the land but doffs his hat to
    him.

As evening shadows lengthen, if the breeze is blowing
    fair,
From beneath his faded jacket he will take with ten-
    der care,
A locket, worn and dented, wherein, framed in curls
    of gold,
Is a face that to the "oldest" never, never will be old,
And his aged eyes grow softer and more tremulous
    his tone
While he tells you how since Anna died he's made
    the trip alone—

And ere the tale's concluded other eyes than his are
    dim—
There's not a drummer but is proud to doff the hat
    to him.

Half the legends of a century, safe hidden in his
    breast,
Come forward at his bidding, in the quaintest lan-
    guage drest;
And he takes such pleasure in them that 'twould really
    be a crime,
Not to listen and applaud them, though 'tis for the
    hundredth time.
He's afloat upon life's ocean like a ship without a
    mast,
All his blessings in the future, all his pleasure in
    the past,
Let us thank him for this lesson, 'tis not strength of
    mind or limb,
But a cheerful sunny spirit wins the hearts of all to
    him.

The sun of life is sinking on the evening of his day,
And his gentle spirit will ere long from earth have
    passed away;
We shall miss the well-known figure from its seat beside
    the door,
And the oldest trav'ler of them all will cheer our
    hearts no more;
But a hundred thousand brothers still his memory
    will keep,
While children laugh, or manhood strives, or broken
    households weep;

And oft on blustering winter nights, about the cheering flame,
Will heads be bowed and speech be hushed at men-
tion of his name.

AN ETCHING

A grateful thought melodious sung
   To every heart if gay or sad;
A spur to speed the sober good,
   A bit to curb the hasting bad;
A bugle blast to him that stays,
   A dreamy harp to him who roams,
A fresh, revolving April day
   In Life's dry summer—this is Holmes.

DEWEY

Not even Caesar, in his height of power,
  Won half so rich a country to his own
As this plain man, whose spirit fills the hour,
  Whose name is known wherever speech is known.
Ten thousand captives Caesar brought to Rome,
Dewey brings naught but broken shackles home.

So is the ancient prophecy fulfilled,
  The heel of love has crushed the serpent's head.
A nation's wealth, a nation's blood, is spilled
  That stranger feet a smoother way may tread.
The treasure Dewey won across the sea
Is heaven's charge—another race is free.

A TROUBLED CONSCIENCE

'Twas but a glance, a hurried glance
  Into a long, low, stifling room,
Where belts and wheels and spindles dance—
  A place of sighs, of prison gloom,
    A murky atmosphere wherein
    Float hope-dead faces, wan and thin.

A plague on shops! I close and close
  My eyes, and yet I cannot sleep
Nor banish from my pillow those
  Who labor for a beggar's keep.
    Is't true that some are born to bear
    And some to ride? Why should I care?

The rose a-bloom on yonder vine
  Has no regret because this tree
Flames in the grate—and both are mine—
  If fortune choose to favor me,
    Must I be robbed of my repose
    Tho' others have nor flame nor rose?

Great God! to breathe in such a place—
  Yet there be those to do this work—
For me I'd welcome death, disgrace,
  Bar mountain pass with brigands dirk,
    Or ere I'd toil in such a den—
    Ah! shall I ever sleep again?

THE COUNTRY TERRIBLE.

There's a country that's dark with innumerable shad-
    ows,
Which over its valleys hang threat'ning and low;
The verdue is withered and dry in its meadows,
Its hills and its forests are bare unto baldness, and
    bitter and black waters flow—
        Yet men will go
        To this land of woe,
Will seek through years for the gate that leads
To this home of pain—by bloodier deeds
Than ever were done by the hands of men,
By treacheries shameful, again and again,
Till they wade knee-deep through a flood of tears,
Destroying the pleasure that Truth endears,
Aye, crush and trample, and cruelly kill,
And hew their way with a giant's will—
A giant's will and a madman's strength,
Till they come, blood-red, to the gate at length,
Which Satan all gleefully backward rolls,
While he bows and smirks to the poor damned souls,
        And they enter in,
        To the hell of sin,
Where want and pestilence, hand in hand,
Go stalking forever—'tis Drunkard's Land.

UNCLE SAM TO THE PHILIPPINES.

All crimson are these hands of mine
  With blood of sons of thine?
Upon thy sands all darkling runs
  The warm, red blood of mine.

Thou art a savage, wild and fierce?
  Lo, I am fiercer still;
Of Roman, Briton, Celt and Dane
  Compounded is my will.

The blood of thine is on my hands?
  The East is streaked with red,
Where coming day has kissed the clouds—
  And thou, thou hast my dead!

I slay and slay? The crowning star
  On Freedom's lifted brow
Was born from flash of clashing steel;
  Shall I desert her now?

If thou art savage, brave, and strong,
  More brave and strong am I;
Thy children's children shall be free,
  Though half my subjects die.

LOVE'S CHILD

The rose that blooms in forest shade
  To please the pretty deer and wild
  Is God's own child;
But thou who on my heart art laid—
Sweet rose of love—alone can cheer
My clouded and forsaken world.
O may thy leaves be never furled,
But hold the smile of Heaven near
That I may see its glory shine—
God's child and mine.

AUTUMN

The leaves are bronze in the autumn air,
Now blushes the apple, and mellow the pear,
The grape hangs purple the vines among,
The brooklets murmur with silv'ry tongue;
The squirrel chatters, low pipes the wren;
The partridge solemnly drums in the fen;
The speck'd quail calls from the orchard wall—
The spell of Autumn is over all.

The fruit peeps forth as the blossoms go—
Your locks, now, white as the April snow,
Were brown in the shadow and gold in the sun
In that first grand Autumn when, Summer done
Our young hearts gladdened with hope's sweet
    wine—
You looked in my eyes and the world was mine,
With never a cloud in the sky above,
And Everywhere wrapped in the robes of love.

O, sweet and tender the words we said,
While laden branches bent down o'erhead—
And your lips met mine—how the ripe fruit roll'd
All about our feet—and the tale was told.
Ah! you were a picture most fair to see,
With cheeks like the bloom of the wild crab tree,
And lips red-ripe and sweeter by far
Than peach and pear and strawberries are.

The years have fled with their joys and pains—
Our cheeks are furrowed with life's fierce rains;
But the path we've trod, as I look behind,
Seems all with beautiful flowers entwined;
Young hearts are beating with hope today,
We've watched and guided in Duty's way,
And the vine-clad mounds, where the daisies nod,
Are only the gateways that lead to God.

The brown nuts open when frost appears,
The dark hair silvers with passing years,
The flowers must wither, the grass lie dead,
Turn feeble and falt'ring the strong man's tread;
The bloom fade out of the smiling rose,
The strong oak bow when the storm king blows;
Some fruits will ripen, some, blighted, fall,
But the leaves of Autumn dance over all.

GRACE DUFFIE BOYLAN

A general with love for sword,
  A comrade always true,
A sun to light the turbid ford
  Were passing through.

A heart wherein a mocking bird
  Has made eternal nest
And sings all song, the latest heard,
  Still seeming best.

A spirit gentle, patient, fond,
  Yet brave as Castelar,
That looks with simple faith beyond
  Hope's farthest star.

Brave, noble heart, through grief to see
  A glad yet peaceful place
Where discord dies for you and me—
  Truth named thee Grace.

THE DUTY SERGEANT

Fate is but a pompous shadow
    That dissolves before "I will,"
Though you follow in the hollow
    You may lead upon the hill.
Stress of strife, or weight of sorrow,
    By these tests alone we know—
Captain he may be tomorrow
    Who today receives the blow.

Patient toil, unending kindness,
    Eyes that see another's grief,
Feet that spring to succor blindness,
    Hands that stretch to give relief.
These are soldiers of a sergeant,
    Duty sergeant strong and grand,
Some day on his shield the argent
    Of commander clear will stand.

THE SPIRIT OF TRUTH.

How strange a spirit this that men
  Are pleased to call Religion.
                          If
'Twere possible to fix upon
The mirror of the mind her form,
With all her features circumscribed—
If this might be and faith still live—
How easy, then, to welcome Truth
And do her timely reverence.
But as the fire-fly in the night,
Flames for an instant and is gone,
So 'tis Religion glows and dies
And glows again, or near or far,
To disappear and leave no trace
Whereby the mind may follow her.
O tantalizing light that leads
The hope into bewilderment,
And to the verge of madness drives
The soul of speculation.
                          She
Who yesterday was queen indeed,
Decked out with jewels, robed in silks,
And in her hand a precious wand,
The scepter of authority,
Today appears clothed all in rags,
And shame-faced seeking darkest way,
And hiding every healthful sign,

Pleads whiningly her woes.

                    One hour
All wisdom, next a grinning clown,
Then seemingly of both combined,
She shows like unregenerate Turk
Still glutinous of evil deeds.
Again a sweet, artistic cheat,
With tear-moist eye, and voice as sad
And plaintive-tuned as dove's amid
The screening boughs of leafy wood, .
Repeating tale so pitious sad
That tears upon the flinty pave
Must give it lasting character.
So comes she in a thousand shapes,
Which, if the least we do deny,
Our conscience pricks us with the thought—
This one was Truth, indeed, and you
Upon the Christ have shut th: door
To your damnation.

                   Comes anon
Another, plain and simply clad,
But beaming sweetly on the world.
In action free as Joan when,
Inspired of God, she fearless faced
The bearded regiments and led
Her legions on to victory.
But sword nor shield doth she require
To give her proper dignity;
The rustle of an angel's wing,
Straight come from heav'n to soothe a grief,
Hath harsher music than her voice

While minist'ring to those distrest.
Lo, from the beaten path of sin
She leads the fallen, tenderly,
And sets the weary, wayward feet
Again on Virtue's dewy green
To wander never more.

                    Her gaze
Is like a sunbeam kissing tombs
Within the confines of a pile
Else wrapped in gloom.

                  So gliding on,
Not prating of what should be done,
Nor questioning why clouds are here,
Or whence they came, she tries all arts
To banish them till skies are bright
And sunshine floods the world.

                    I care
Not how she may be gowned, if silk
Or cotton clothe her, she's not robed
With purpose to betray.

                    I know
The dome of heaven's none too high
To roof the church wherein she learned
Her saving creed; to cheer, not chide,
Her simple article of faith.
I stand uncovered where she is,
Because I know from these, her works,
That Christ hath triumphed o'er the grave
And lives to bless and save the world.

THE END